A Beautiful Mess

WEEKDAY
WEEKEND

A Beautiful Mess

WEEKDAY
WEEKEND

How to live a healthy veggie life
...and still eat treats

Text and photographs by
Emma Chapman and Elsie Larson

CHRONICLE BOOKS
SAN FRANCISCO

Library of Congress Cataloging-in-Publication Data

Names: Larson, Elsie, author | Chapman, Emma, author.
Title: A beautiful mess : weekday weekend /
text and photographs by Elsie Larson and Emma Chapman.
Description: San Francisco : Chronicle Books, [2017]
Identifiers: LCCN 2016053237 | ISBN 9781452154718 (hc : alk. paper)
Subjects: LCSH: Vegetarian cooking. | LCGFT: Cookbooks.
Classification: LCC TX837 .L258 2017 | DDC 641.5/636—dc23 LC record
available at https://lccn.loc.gov/2016053237

Manufactured in China.

Prop and food styling by Elsie Larson and Emma Chapman
Designed by Alice Chau
Cover and page 12 designed by Mara Dockery
Photos on pages 2, 8, 19, and 204 by Alyssa Rosenheck

10 9 8 7 6 5 4 3 2

Chronicle books and gifts are available at special quantity discounts to corporations, professional associations, literacy programs, and other organizations. For details and discount information, please contact our premiums department at corporatesales@chroniclebooks.com or at 1-800-759-0190.

Chronicle Books LLC
680 Second Street
San Francisco, California 94107
www.chroniclebooks.com

We dedicate this book to our mother, Elizabeth Chapman.
She is a constant source of inspiration, love, and passion in our lives.
She has and continues to teach us to live a creative life without fear,
to take on projects that scare us, and to try and enjoy every meal
that we are lucky enough to have along the way.

Contents

snacks & sweets **150**

drinks **178**

introduction

If you are like us, you love food. You might not plan out every meal, but you do look forward to the next one. We love the fabulous variety out there—in the color, shape, texture, and taste of foods, and in the techniques from all around the world for preparing them. We love trying new foods. We love exploring new restaurants. We love cooking delicious meals at home. We love it all!

But of course food isn't just about flavor, or the experience of eating it. Food is also what sustains us and is the huge core factor in our overall health, and this can feel really daunting at times—especially in this era, when a proliferation of information creates a dizzying swirl of choices. Are we eating enough healthy foods? Should we be eating more organic, local, seasonal, non-GMO, gluten-free, vegan, low-calorie, low-fat, low-sodium, sugar-free foods?! The answers for how to eat healthy can feel far away and ever changing. It's enough to make you want to throw your hands in the air in frustration . . . and then promptly have a brownie and glass of wine for dinner, thinking you'll worry about it tomorrow.

Not that we've ever done this.

Over the past few years, it was this very frustration that pushed us to try to develop a new approach to figuring out what we should be eating. And that's how we came up with a simple system we called "weekday/weekend" eating. It's easy to follow: there are only five "rules." And it's sustainable: you could eat this way forever, if you wanted to. We recommend, however, that the first time you try it, just do it for 4 to 6 weeks. Meant to be both a changeup of your routine and doable for anyone, Weekday Weekend is designed to help you become more aware of your eating habits and learn more about easy options for improving them, without making you feel like if you don't know everything, you can't be a part of the healthy-eating club. Starting with a realistic timeframe will support the "no intimidation" premise of our program while still giving you enough time to see some change in your habits.

Most importantly, Weekday Weekend eating is built for variety and has plenty of space for indulgences. We want to make food choices that will promote a long, healthy life—but with room for treats, because life's too short to go without those!

THE 5 RULES

1. eat a variety of foods

2. no refined or artificial sugars or sweeteners

3. no refined white flour or white rice

4. no dairy

5. no alcohol

WEEKEND:

NO RULES!!!

The Weekday Weekend concept is simple. For 5 days a week, we eat according to 5 rules.

1. eat a variety of foods.

Eat the whole rainbow of colors, and eat seasonally when you can. Every different color in food (including whites and browns) indicates a different array of vitamins, minerals, phytochemicals, enzymes, and other elements that speak to our bodies on the cellular level—and the bigger the range you select from, the more benefits from nature's bounty you're reaping. Eating seasonally makes sense on many levels, including carbon footprint and supporting small farms and your local economy—and in terms of health benefits, of course, produce contains the most nutrients when it is at its peak of ripeness. Plus, paying attention to color and what emerges directly from the source season by season makes shopping, cooking, and eating fun—it should never be boring.

2. no refined or artificial sugars or sweeteners.

We're mainly talking about refined white sugar or all those hidden sugars that are often sneaked into our foods, such as yogurt, bread, and fruit juices. Naturally occurring sugars are OK; in this cookbook, we mainly use fruits, honey, pure maple syrup, or a little bit of molasses to sweeten weekday recipes (each choice stems from the subtle note they can add to the flavor of the finished dish, as well). The goal here is not to demonize sugar. We love sugar! We just don't want it to be a large part of our daily diet, but rather something we enjoy as a treat now and again.

3. no refined white flour or white rice.

Whole grains are welcomed; if you're new to this way of eating, you might be surprised just how many whole grains there are to enjoy! In this cookbook we will mainly be focused on recipes that use 100 percent whole wheat flour, oats, brown rice, black rice, quinoa, and spelt flour. But there are SO many more whole grains that can be enjoyed while you try out Weekday Weekend. If you want to challenge yourself even more after trying Weekday Weekend you might consider going gluten-free or even grain-free for a while just to see how you feel. But for our purposes we're going to start simply by focusing on avoiding white flour and white rice.

4. no dairy.

It's just too easy to douse everything in butter and cheese, isn't it? The good news is there are SO many other options out there. You can still enjoy soy or nut milks, soy or coconut yogurt, or vegan butters or cheeses so long as they do not contain added sugars (see rule #2) You can also use any oil you prefer for cooking; we mainly use olive oil throughout this cookbook but feel free to try others for variety, like coconut oil. We'll also show you how to make your own mayo so you won't be missing out on having something decadent and creamy now and again for sauces or dressings.

5. no alcohol.

Extracts are OK; we're talking about cooking with a substantial amount of wine or enjoying a cocktail every day.

A Beautiful Mess

Those are your menu guidelines for your weekday life: four No's and one big, adventurous Yes! What five days your weekdays fall on is up to you and your schedule. Probably for most of us it's going to be Monday through Friday, but if you've got a weird work schedule, feel free to adjust this. The important thing is that for the majority of the week, we are going to seek out lots of super-healthy stuff to fill our lives with.

The second part of the formula is as important as the first: For two days a week—during your weekend, wherever it may fall—we eat whatever we want to. This helps erase any sense of deprivation and in fact ups the empowerment as it gives us a break from any extra mental energy it may take to keep an eye on the weekday rules. Part of the goal in Weekday Weekend is to educate yourself as you go along. You'll be reading lots of food labels and trying to eat a big variety of foods that may be in season. This takes time and extra effort and we get it—you're busy with work, family, and life as well. So work hard at Weekday Weekend for five days and then take a little break as you gear up for the next week. This can also help us navigate social events that may lean heavily toward foods and drinks that don't work well during the week. It's OK to enjoy these moments in life as they arise, but they should not be the everyday norm. And even on the weekends keep in mind that we still always try to keep moderation in mind. If you've been craving a brownie and a beer all week long, then the weekend is the time to indulge; just don't go overboard. We should be in charge of our food choices, not the other way around. #thestruggleisreal.

That's it. That's the whole manifesto. You just have to remember five things and then go forth and figure out the rest. Read all packaging labels. Google things that are unfamiliar and/or unpronounceable to you. If you're unsure—just do your best and know that we are rooting for you! You never need to feel bad when engaged in the challenge. The goal is to learn, try new

things, and grow in our healthy eating knowledge base. Stay curious!

You may have noticed that we don't mention meat in the Weekday Weekend rules, and that the cookbook you're holding doesn't include any meat-based recipes. What's up with that? Well, one of the added benefits of taking the Weekday Weekend eating challenge is that you're going to be eating a mostly plant-based diet. If you already happen to be vegetarian or vegan, obviously this part of the regimen won't be any different; but for everyone else, we recommend you give meatless, or mostly meatless, a try. But feel free to eat some meat now and again, if you want. The option can be especially helpful if you are in Weekday mode and end up at a restaurant that just doesn't have a lot of selections that can work for you. If you do choose to eat meat, we strongly recommend you seek out sustainably raised meats, preferably local, and avoid anything produced from companies that use factory-farming practices. If you haven't heard of that term before, just Google "factory farming" and start there. There are also lots of great documentaries out there that speak to this topic more generally; one we loved is *Forks Over Knives*. If you don't know the practices or reputation of a producer, get on Google and do some research. Again, stay curious, people!

We believe that anyone can eat healthily and that you don't need an advanced degree to be able to make good choices. But we also recognize that health-care professionals can be a GREAT source of information as we look to expand our healthy-eating knowledge. That is why we had two nutritionists work on this book alongside us. They contributed a wealth of additional information and expert advice. We learned so much from them during the course of writing this book, and are so happy to have them be part of this project.

who is weekday weekend for?

Everyone. It's not a detox or crash diet. It's meant to be a sustainable way to make healthy food choices and to continue to learn over the course of your life.

how should you use this book?

There are two main options:

1. Take the Weekday Weekend eating challenge.

Decide if you want to try the program for 4, 5, or 6 weeks at time, and go for it. Follow the 5 rules during the week and enjoy your weekends. See how you feel. Did you end up having more energy? Did you sleep better? Did you feel like your learned more or found new foods that you now enjoy? Did you discover you were a little bit addicted to sugar?

You can use this eating challenge anytime, like a reset button.

Once you get the hang of Weekday Weekend using this book, if you find it suits you, try subsequent rounds adding other challenges. Setting mini challenges for yourself is a great way to keep things feeling fresh and to stay engaged. Some options to consider:

- Start every day with something green. We've included a few green smoothie recipes in our weekday breakfast section but other examples could include: a spinach omelette, broccoli quiche, or a breakfast salad (greens and fruit—yum!).

- Make a goal to drink more water (especially if you don't already drink enough; you'll find more information on page 180 and some inspiration on page 183).

- Remove all sweeteners from your weekday diet, including the ones we allow in this cookbook.

- Go grain-free.

- Eat at least one raw meal a day.

- Research the benefits of eating organic or avoiding GMOs.

There are endless ways to challenge yourself if you want to take Weekday Weekend eating to the next level.

2. Just use this like a normal cookbook.

Maybe you don't want to try the full program, but you like the idea of having a mix of healthy and healthy-but-indulgent recipes in a single volume. This cookbook totally fits the bill. As with almost any cookbook, try the recipes for the first time verbatim, so you can glean all the delicious and nutritious know-how built into the original intentions. Then if you want to change it up, go for it! Adapt away.

No matter if you are jumping head first into Weekday Weekend eating or you picked up this book simply because you liked the photos—either way, we're glad you are here! We hope this book will be a resource to encourage you on your own healthy-eating journey. It's been immensely important to us, and we feel so honored to get to share it with you. Thank you for reading.

a note from our nutritionists

Hi! We're Lindsey and Sarah, registered dietitian/nutritionists here to help you on your journey through this wonderful cookbook. The first thing you may be wondering is: What is a registered dietitian/nutritionist and how is that different from a nutritionist? A registered dietitian/nutritionist (RDN) is a certified nutrition expert. Certification and expert status aren't easy to come by. We pulled numerous all-nighters in college cramming for biochemistry exams; toiled at unpaid, exhausting internships; passed challenging board exams; and we must complete continuing education as long as we stay in practice.

Technically, anyone can claim to be a nutritionist, but may lack the knowledge needed to dish out professional nutrition advice. This is not to say that dietitians are the only ones with any nutrition know-how, but that RDN stamp means we have a core understanding of how the body works and how the things we put in our mouths can affect our bodies. Being an RDN also means we keep up with new research and discoveries in the ever-changing field of nutrition and can transform all of that information into a personalized eating plan.

We got into "the biz" in the first place because we love food. Eating is our jam.

Nutrition myths and trends run rampant. Whether it's cabbage soup, HCG, or the "chew-don't-swallow" diet, we've encountered a lot of "interesting" diets over the years. What we really love about Weekday/Weekend eating is that it's not a diet at all. It's a simple way of eating that is sustainable for the long haul. The recipes are delicious and the "weekend" days allow for the flexibility life requires. The weekday recipes are not crazy restrictive, but are in fact indulgent—full of crunch, creaminess, big on flavor—while still healthy. We don't believe

in crash diets or quick fixes. We endorse moderation, clean eating, and making overall healthy lifestyle changes (read: not dieting) like those suggested here. We also recommend you eat real food. This bring up another term that may require clarification: What is real food? It's what your grandma ate: lettuce, not veggie straws, fruit, not fruit-flavored candy, eggs, not egg substitute. Grow a garden. Plant some herbs. When grocery shopping, read the food label and throw out anything that has words you can't pronounce; these are little red flags declaring, "This is not a real food!" A good rule of thumb is to aim for foods that have five or fewer ingredients listed on the label.

It's apparent a lot of time and love was put into these recipes. In keeping with the care Emma and Elsie gave to this book, we would also like to encourage you, the reader/eater, to begin practicing a little something called mindful eating. Mindful eating is the art of truly appreciating every aspect of your food. There are so many benefits to eating mindfully, not only for your personal enjoyment but also your health. By taking the time to slow down—taste, chew, smell, concentrate on eating and appreciate your food—you will not only experience more satisfaction, but will also avoid the urge to overeat. This is an ancient practice with age-old benefits, yet one that is so needed in today's fast-paced, plugged-in world. If you haven't researched mindful eating we encourage you to do so—just not on your phone while you're eating because, you know, that kind of defeats the whole purpose.

Now, on to the "rules" you just read, and why we think they're so great.

1. eat a variety of foods. eat all sorts of colors and eat seasonally when you can.

Repeat after us: "A colorful meal, better you shall feel." Everything sounds easier when it rhymes, right? Unfortunately, this one can be tricky to put into action, but is so important. Eating a variety of real, colorful foods helps to ensure that you are getting all of the nutrients your body needs to stay in tip-top shape. Colorful fruits and vegetables are two foods that are oh-so neglected in the modern diet and it can take some effort on your part to seek them out. Visit your local farmer's market or join a Community Supported Agriculture (CSA) group. Search store ads for produce sales and choose those that are seasonal (snaped.fns.usda.gov has a good list). These will be less expensive and generally have a higher nutrient content than fruits or vegetables out of season. Utilize the recipes in this book to go out of your comfort zone and try something you have never tried before. You might just find that you like it.

2. no refined or artificial sugars/sweeteners.

Sugar has as many different names as Beyoncé has platinum hits (sucrose, fructose, corn syrup, high-fructose corn syrup, dextrose, rice syrup, maltose, to name just a few) and just because something is labeled as "natural" or "unrefined" does not automatically mean it is good for you. Quick clarification: here we are talking about sweeteners that add calories, not the artificial calorie-free ones found in diet drinks (see Weekday Drinks for our take on those). When it comes to sweeteners the moral of the story is that "sugar is sugar" no matter which one you choose. Sugar is addictive. No joke. This means your body can crave sugar like it does other addictive substances. Moderation is key to fending off cravings. A good rule is to keep added sugar to fewer than 10 percent of total calories each day and less is better. For example, if you need 2000 calories a day, you should keep added sugar to 12 teaspoons or less per day. A 20-ounce regular soda contains 16 teaspoons of added sugar—more than you should have for the whole day! You can see how easy it is to get too much if you don't keep an eye out.

You will find that the weekday recipes utilize small amounts of unrefined sugar in the form of honey, maple syrup, coconut sugar, and molasses. While, strictly speaking, any altering done after collecting puts that food into the processed category, we feel that these sugars are minimally altered (for example maple syrup is boiled), keeping them in a more natural state, and making them your best choice for sweetener. An added bonus is these sweeteners are more likely to be found in unprocessed foods, so sticking to this rule helps you to eat more real food.

3. no refined white flour or white rice. whole grains are welcomed.

Quinoa, wild rice, whole oats, whole wheat, barley, whole-grain brown rice—these are just a few of the many delicious whole grains you'll see incorporated into the weekday recipes. It can be tricky to identify what constitutes a whole-grain or whole-wheat product, so here are some tips: A whole grain literally means the entire grain is preserved, no amount of milling or refining has separated the bran, germ, and endosperm, which is where all the healthy B vitamins, fats, antioxidants, and minerals are found. If the grain has been processed (cracked, crushed, rolled, extruded) but is still intact, the food should be as nutritious as what was supplied by the original grain seed. Double check the ingredient list on the food label and make sure the word "whole" is included to be sure it's the real deal. (Note: Foods that read multigrain, wheatberry, or 100 percent wheat are usually not really whole-grain and not your healthiest sources of fiber, vitamins, and minerals.)

Cooking with whole grains might require a little bit of practice on your part. We'd be lying if we said there weren't a few burnt pans or soggy pots of mush in our kitchens before we perfected the art of cooking grains al dente. But once you master the art of cooking whole grains properly, your heart, body, and mind will thank you.

4. no dairy.

While we do believe that quality dairy can be included in a healthy diet, we agree that it can be easy to overindulge. Many of the dairy products available in grocery stores (low-fat yogurts, processed cheeses) contain added sugars and other junk that is not good for us. For the weekends, we recommend picking whole-fat, locally sourced dairy products that do not contain added ingredients. One thing to keep in mind is that dairy is a big source of calcium, so when you're excluding it during the week make sure to include other good sources of calcium, such as spinach, arugula, broccoli, figs, sesame seeds, molasses, and tahini.

5. no alcohol.

The recommendations for moderate drinking are for no more than two drinks a day for men and one a day for women (not fair). The weekday guidelines take that a little further. Excessive alcohol contains empty calories and has damaging effects on our bodies, so the bottom line is that less is more. Let's instead focus our attention on consuming plenty of water during the week so we can guiltlessly kick back on the weekends.

In a nutshell, the problem with a traditional "diet" is that it is not sustainable. Each and every one of us must eat to live. A meal should be both satisfying and nourishing, otherwise, we'll find ourselves depleted both physically and emotionally. When we set out to permanently eliminate something we enjoy, human nature will eventually have us crawling back for more, therein kicking off a vicious cycle of guilt, remorse, and self doubt. That's no fun, so let's avoid that. Think of Weekday Weekend eating as a lifestyle change. Give it a go for 4 to 6 weeks; chances are you won't look back.

break

kfasts

WEEKDAY

Breakfast is touted as the most important meal of the day, but for various reasons, it can become quite stressful. I find that I often have very little time to devote to this important moment of the day. I tend to get stuck making meals that come together fast, or that are able to travel with me, or that I can literally eat on the run. Because we know many of you are in a similar boat, we trust you'll be happy to see that most of our weekday breakfasts can be thrown together in a quick 10 to 20 minutes—without sacrificing flavor, nutrition, or comfort.

from the nutritionists

We. Love. Breakfast. And it is one of the three most important meals of the day. Joking aside, there is something to be said about starting your day off with the right blend of yummy and nutritious that can really get you going. The great thing about the weekday breakfast recipes is they are quick and portable, while still managing to pack in plenty of good stuff along the way.

Let's talk smoothies. The recipes you'll find here highlight a super-delicious way to get in your fruit and veggie servings. Keep in mind that the average adult should get at least 2 cups of fruit and 2½ to 3 cups of vegetables each day. The Mojito Green Smoothie has 1½ cups of fruit and 4 cups of veggies! That's almost all your F and V's for the day! The Super Food Smoothie Bowl has so many crazy-nutritious ingredients we lost count. Blueberries and goji berries are full of vitamins, antioxidants, and phytochemicals—the stuff in fruit that is touted as health-inducing and cancer-preventing and we just can't seem to recreate in a supplement. Spirulina is a type of algae that may have anti-viral, anticancer, and immune system–boosting benefits. While the jury is still out on some of this, we do know that spirulina is chock full of vitamins, minerals, and protein. So eat on!

On to whole grains. You'll see whole oats, brown rice, and chickpeas are used in several weekday recipes. These are great ways to get in fiber, which helps stave off those mid-morning cravings, AND chickpeas double as a vegetable—score! Whole grains are also full of vitamins and minerals like magnesium, phosphorus, copper, manganese, selenium, and B vitamins. When choosing bread, make sure it is a whole-grain option—this means it has the words "100 percent whole grain" or "100 percent whole wheat" written somewhere on the package and the word "whole" is listed before the first ingredient. And don't be fooled by the color; some light colored breads may be whole wheat and

some dark colored breads may be refined (100 percent white whole wheat is a real thing). We really like sprouted grain breads like Ezekiel bread, but, for some, it takes some getting used to. Don't be discouraged if you don't love whole-wheat bread the first time—like wine, it's an acquired taste. Buy different brands and keep on trying it—you'll be surprised what your taste buds will tell you!

You may have noticed that unsweetened almond milk and coconut milk are included in several recipes in keeping with the no-dairy weekday rule. As dietitians, we get a lot of questions about how these items compare to cow's milk. The biggest surprise for many is the difference in protein content—both almond and coconut have about 1 gram per cup versus cow's milk with 8 grams. If you'd like to get more protein you can add foods like eggs, nuts, seeds, chickpeas, hummus, or nut butters as a side dish to those recipes that don't already have it!

miso granola

MAKES ABOUT THREE CUPS;
SERVES SIX TO EIGHT

One thing you should know about me before you make this great granola recipe with a salty Asian twist is, I like my granola quite toasty. Not burnt—but on its way. I think it takes on much more flavor that way. I also just plain love this rendition, as the granola is both sweet and savory, and makes for a fantastic, satisfying, and quick breakfast folded into some coconut yogurt or with almond milk poured over. Add some fresh fruit and you're in business, either way.

⅓ cup [80 ml] olive oil

2½ Tbsp pure maple syrup

2 Tbsp miso paste (see Note)

2 cups [200 g] rolled oats

1 cup [120 g] sliced almonds

⅓ cup [25 g] unsweetened
 coconut flakes

½ tsp salt

Preheat the oven to 350°F [180°C]. Line a baking sheet with parchment paper or a silicone baking mat.

In a glass measuring cup, stir together the olive oil, maple syrup, and miso until well combined. Set aside.

Put the oats in a small bowl. In another small bowl, stir together the almonds and coconut flakes.

Pour half of the liquid ingredients over the oats and half over the almonds and coconut flakes. Stir each well, so that all the pieces get thoroughly coated.

Spread the oats in a single layer on the prepared baking sheet. Bake for 10 minutes, then remove from the oven and scatter the almond and coconut mixture on the pan. Sprinkle everything with the salt, stir well, and spread in a single layer again. Bake until the granola looks very toasted (a few pieces of the coconut flakes may even look like they're burning), 10 to 12 minutes longer. Remove from the oven and let cool.

Store at room temperature in a glass jar, tightly covered with a lid, or in a big plastic zippered bag for up to 2 weeks. (Mine never lasts longer than a week, though, as I LOVE sprinkling it over smoothie bowls—see pages 29–32—or eating it at any time of day when I need a quick snack or small meal.)

Note: Miso, a classic ingredient in Japanese cooking, is made primarily from fermented soybeans, which give it a rich, salty, umami flavor. Often found in paste form, it can be added to soups, broths, marinades, or any time you want to add a deeper, more complex layer of flavor to recipes (miso caramel, yum!). Miso is a powerful antioxidant, rich in zinc, copper, and manganese, and can be found in almost all major grocery stores and at your local Asian market.

A Beautiful Mess

steel-cut oats with sweet potato and pumpkin seeds

SERVES ONE

This recipe glamorizes hearty oats with crunchy, nutty pumpkin seeds and mashed sweet potato. Now, you might be thinking, "What gives? I thought you said I could make this in a hurry—I don't have time to bake and mash a sweet potato every morning!" I hear you. I don't either. It's make-ahead magic; I bake and mash a sweet potato or two over the weekend and store them in an airtight container in the refrigerator to use in bowls of oatmeal, sandwiches, or my Garlicky Sweet Potato Bites (page 134) during the week. Trust me; they keep beautifully in the fridge for days. You can also freeze mashed sweet potatoes in easy-to-use portions in ice-cube trays, if you find that you're reaching for them often and would like a big batch to use for weeks on end.

1 cup [240 ml] water

Sea salt

⅓ cup [55 g] steel-cut oats

2 Tbsp pumpkin seeds

1 Tbsp sunflower seeds

2 tsp sesame seeds

¼ cup [60 g] mashed baked sweet potato (see Note, page 134)

1 to 2 Tbsp pure maple syrup

In a saucepan, heat the water and a pinch of salt over high heat until almost boiling. Add the oats, stir once, cover, and reduce the heat to maintain a simmer. Cook until tender, 12 to 15 minutes.

Meanwhile, toast all of the seeds in a small, dry skillet over medium heat, stirring constantly, just until fragrant and the sesame seeds begin to brown, 1 to 2 minutes. Remove from the heat, pour onto a plate immediately, and set aside.

When the oats are cooked, add the mashed sweet potato to the pan and stir to mix well. Add maple syrup to taste and a little more salt, if needed. Pour into your bowl, top with the toasted seeds, and serve immediately.

smoothies and smoothie bowls

EACH RECIPE SERVES ONE

When it comes to morning smoothies, I think it's very important to ENJOY your routine. If you don't enjoy it, you'll end up skipping it. I developed these smoothie recipes to be enticing, refreshing, and easy— in the time it takes you to make your morning coffee, you can have a delicious, nutrient-filled smoothie to start your day. If you like the simplicity of drinking your breakfast, stick to smoothies; smoothie bowls invite you to sit down and enjoy your smoothie with crunchy nuts and seeds, more ripe fruit, and a whole world of toppings.

To make these smoothie and smoothie bowls, pile all of the ingredients into a high-powered blender and blend until creamy and completely—as the name says—smooth. (Don't stint on time; with denser ingredients, this can take several minutes. When blending leafy greens add them first with other ingredients on top before blending to encourage them to sink to the bottom and get fully blended.)

mojito green smoothie

As the name suggests this smoothie has some tropical flavors paired with mint that make it super refreshing. This is a really great green smoothie recipe for all you green smoothie skeptics out there, as the flavor boost from the fruits and mint help to make it a bit more palatable if you aren't used to blended greens. I hope I'm not scaring you off as this truly is a super delicious and nutritious way to start your day.

4 cups [80 g] fresh spinach

1 frozen banana

½ cup [70 g] frozen
  pineapple chunks

10 fresh mint leaves

1 cup [240 ml] unsweetened
  coconut milk

1 Tbsp fresh lime juice

hidden spinach chocolate smoothie

Green smoothies are incredibly good for you, but sometimes a green drink doesn't sound appealing. For days like that, I make this "hidden spinach" smoothie that's excitingly like a chocolate shake. Indulge!

2 cups [40 g] fresh spinach

1 frozen banana

1 Tbsp unsweetened black or regular
  Dutch-processed cocoa powder

1 cup [240 ml] unsweetened
  almond milk

½ cup [120 g] coconut or
  other non-dairy yogurt

1 Tbsp coconut sugar

superfood smoothie bowl

This recipe combines a bunch of my favorite superfoods in one tasty bowl. Make this for yourself and pretend like you're having breakfast at a cool LA juice bar next to Gwen Stefani. Dare to dream. Pour into a bowl and top with more of your favorite fresh fruit and toasted nuts.

1 cup [140 g] frozen blueberries

1 cup [140 g] frozen
  pineapple chunks

1 frozen banana

¼ cup [35 g] dehydrated goji berries

¼ cup [20 g] unsweetened
  coconut flakes

1 Tbsp chia seeds

½ tsp spirulina

1 cup [240 ml] unsweetened
  almond milk

dark chocolate–peanut butter smoothie bowl

For a truly indulgent treat, this is my favorite smoothie bowl. It can TOTALLY substitute as ice cream on a weekday.

2 frozen bananas

2 Tbsp Dutch-processed cocoa powder

2 Tbsp unsweetened, natural peanut butter

1 Tbsp raw honey

1 cup [240 ml] unsweetened almond milk

piña colada–papaya smoothie bowl

This is my favorite tropical smoothie bowl of all time. The flavors are so evocative; you'll feel like you're on vacation in the Virgin Islands... even on a Tuesday. Pour into a bowl, or if you want to multiply the recipe and wow guests, serve in hollowed-out fresh pineapple half shells. (In that case, substitute the frozen pineapple with fresh and add a handful of ice.) Top with dehydrated goji berries, coconut flakes, and/or whatever fresh fruit is in season.

1 frozen banana

1 cup [140 g] frozen pineapple chunks

½ cup [80 g] dehydrated papaya

½ cup [40 g] unsweetened coconut flakes

½ cup [120 g] coconut or other non-dairy yogurt

½ cup [120 g] unsweetened almond milk

kale frittata with creamy lemon sauce

SERVES TWO TO THREE

Simple but substantial, this frittata might make an even better dinner than breakfast—but I love breakfast for dinner, and vice versa! Filled with lightly cooked kale and toothsome potatoes and topped with a lemon sauce that delivers a bright pop of citrus, this healthy weekday dish seems decadent.

4 large eggs

⅓ cup [80 ml] unsweetened almond or cashew milk

Salt and freshly ground black pepper

3 tsp olive oil

1 cup [15 g] chopped kale

1 red potato, peeled and cubed

1 clove garlic, minced

FOR THE LEMON SAUCE:

2 large egg yolks

2 tsp water

2 Tbsp coconut oil

3 Tbsp fresh lemon juice

¼ tsp cayenne pepper

½ tsp arrowroot powder (see Note, page 35)

Preheat the oven to 350°F [180°C].

In a bowl, whisk together the eggs and almond milk. Season with a little salt and black pepper and set aside.

In an 8-in [20-cm] cast-iron or other oven-safe skillet over medium heat, heat 1 tsp of the olive oil. Add the kale and sauté until it begins to soften and turn a darker shade of green, 1 to 2 minutes. Transfer to a plate lined with paper towels to remove excess moisture.

Return the same skillet to medium heat and warm the remaining 2 tsp olive oil. Add the potato and cook for about 5 minutes, tossing occasionally and scraping the pan bottom so the potato doesn't stick. Once the potato has softened, add the garlic and cook for another 1 minute.

continued . . .

Return the kale to the pan and stir to mix well. Pour the egg mixture over everything and use your spoon to tuck the potato pieces and kale into the egg so that they are all covered as much as possible. Reduce the heat to low and cook, without disturbing, for another 2 to 3 minutes, until the eggs begin to pull away from the sides of the skillet. Carefully transfer the pan to the oven and bake until the center looks set, about 15 minutes.

Meanwhile, make the lemon sauce: In a small saucepan, combine the egg yolks and water. Warm over very low heat, whisking constantly. Add the coconut oil, 1 Tbsp at a time, whisking to help it melt into the yolks. Whisk in the lemon juice and cayenne. At this point, the sauce will have a very thin consistency. Continuing to cook over low heat, sift the arrowroot powder into the sauce through a fine-mesh sieve. (Be patient while sifting; you want to avoid creating lumps in the sauce.) Keep whisking over low heat; soon the sauce will begin to thicken up. Just before it gets too thick (it should still be loose enough to drizzle easily), remove the sauce from the heat and transfer to a bowl.

When the frittata is done, let cool slightly, then run a butter knife around the edges to loosen. Place a large plate upside down over the pan and carefully invert to unmold the frittata onto the plate. Drizzle the sauce over the top. Cut into 4 wedges, arrange 2 wedges on each of 2 individual plates, and serve immediately. If you are serving 3 you can cut into 3 wedges and you may consider serving alongside some hash browns or a small salad—up to you.

Note: Arrowroot powder is a naturally gluten-free thickening agent made from ground dry arrowroot, a starch extracted from a tropical tuber or rhizome. Often used in jellies and glazes or as a replacement for cornstarch, arrowroot works best in recipes that use cold or freezing temperatures to thicken. Arrowroot powder is often used in recipes for homemade infant formula as it is much more nutritious than other starch alternatives, containing B vitamins, folate, and minerals such as copper, iron, magnesium, phosphorus, and zinc. You can find arrowroot powder at specialty health food stores or online.

brown rice and roasted banana porridge

SERVES ONE

This recipe is rice pudding–esque—except it's really good for you. Score! Pulsing the brown rice in a blender helps to cut down on cooking time, and also creates a creamier texture. (If you want to keep a bit of bite to your rice, pulse less.) I also sometimes like to add a handful of Smoky Coconut Flakes (page 129) or chopped nuts. If you find yourself making this recipe often, grind a larger batch of brown rice all at once and store an airtight container for up to 3 months. This step will save you even more time on busy mornings.

⅓ cup [65 g] brown rice
½ cup [120 ml] water
½ cup [120 ml] unsweetened almond milk
1 ripe banana
1 Tbsp pure maple syrup, plus more to taste
Sea salt
¼ tsp ground cinnamon

Preheat the oven to 400°F [200°C]. Line a baking sheet with parchment paper, or grease lightly with oil.

In a high-powered blender or food processor, pulse the brown rice until it is a uniform coarse, grainy texture (think: almost sand or very small pebbles). In a small saucepan, combine the water and almond milk and heat over high heat until almost boiling. Add the ground brown rice, cover, and reduce the heat to maintain a gentle simmer. Cook until tender, about 12 minutes.

Meanwhile, cut the banana in half lengthwise and place on the prepared baking sheet. Brush the banana with the maple syrup and sprinkle with a pinch of sea salt. Roast until the color has darkened and the edges appear a bit shriveled, about 12 minutes. Remove from the oven, let cool slightly, and cut into chunks.

When the rice is done, remove from the heat and stir in the cinnamon. Scoop into a serving bowl and top with the roasted banana. Drizzle a little more maple syrup on top, if you like, and serve immediately.

spelt-zucchini-carob waffles

MAKES THREE TO FOUR WAFFLES; SERVES TWO TO THREE

Spelt is a whole grain with a subtle nutty flavor that makes these waffles unique. We will also whip the egg whites before incorporating as this will help our final waffle texture be a bit more soft and airy. Add shredded zucchini and chopped carob or unsweetened dark chocolate chips and you've got a hot and crispy, flavor-packed, whole-grain breakfast.

Coconut whipped cream is easy to make and really tasty: use a whisk or electric mixer to whip chilled coconut milk (I keep a can in my refrigerator). Lightly sweeten with honey or add a pinch of salt, cinnamon, or a few drops of vanilla extract, then use to top waffles or grilled fruit.

1 cup plus 2 Tbsp [130 g] whole grain spelt flour

1½ Tbsp aluminum-free baking powder

⅛ tsp salt

2 large eggs, separated

¾ cup [180 ml] unsweetened almond or cashew milk

2 Tbsp olive oil

½ tsp pure vanilla extract

⅓ cup [60 g] shredded and drained zucchini

1 Tbsp chopped carob chips (see Note)

Coconut whipped cream, natural nut butters, fresh fruit, or pure maple syrup for serving (optional, see recipe introduction)

Preheat a waffle iron. In a large bowl, whisk together the flour, baking powder, and salt. Add the egg yolks, almond milk, olive oil, and vanilla to the dry ingredients and stir until just combined and nearly no lumps remain. Fold in the zucchini and carob chips and set aside.

In a clean bowl, whisk the egg whites until very foamy and soft peaks form. Using a rubber spatula, fold the egg whites into the batter, just until no big white streaks remain. (Be sure not to overmix here; the egg whites give the waffles a little lift from all the air you just incorporated into them.)

Scoop the waffle batter into the hot iron, ¼ cup [60 ml] at a time, and cook according to the manufacturer's instructions. Served topped with coconut whipped cream, nut butter, fresh fruit, and/or maple syrup, as you like.

Note: You can also use unsweetened dark chocolate chips, but if you do, increase the amount to 2 Tbsp. Carob is a very bold flavor, so we use less in order not to overwhelm the recipe.

toasts
(weekday and weekend)

Welcome to the world of toasts. If you haven't yet discovered the joys of a hot, crispy, nutty slab of bread spread with a meal-worthy second layer, you're in for a treat that will serve you (literally) for many a perfect breakfast—and an endless possibility for toppings lends them equally well to snacks or light lunches. A logical progression of the classic toast and butter and jam, you can make them whatever you want, according to time of day, time of year, and what might be in season, all in minutes.

In the pages below are half a dozen recipes for the toast of the toasts, featuring homemade spreads and an updated classic composition or two. The first four are for weekdays and three more indulgent recipes are for the weekend. The homemade spreads make enough to cover a few rounds of toasting; the composed toasts can be multiplied for as many eager diners as you have lining up at your table. Use good-quality whole-grain toast for all (we like Ezekiel brand), or make your own, like our Whole-Wheat English Muffins (page 46). The weekend Caprese toast indulges in a traditional white Italian loaf to match the ingredients.

cashew cream and berry toast

Sweet and creamy on hot toast, this spread makes the perfect weekday replacement for French toast. Add a few more berries and an extra drizzle of honey, if you like.

Combine 1 cup [140 g] raw cashews, soaked in water to cover for 1 hour and drained; ¼ cup [30 g] fresh or thawed frozen raspberries (if frozen thaw thoroughly first); 2 Tbsp safflower oil; and 1 Tbsp raw honey in a blender and blend to a completely smooth purée. Store any leftovers in an airtight container in the refrigerator for up to 3 days.

A Beautiful Mess

fried egg and avocado toast

This breakfast combo has become a new classic. So good and perfectly satisfying, it only takes about 10 minutes to make. For an even more no-fuss version, skip the egg and top with sprouts or toasted sunflower seeds.

Spread ½ tsp store-bought (no sugar added) or homemade (page 125) mayonnaise thinly on warm toast. Scoop ½ ripe avocado on top and mash to cover the toast evenly. Sprinkle with pink Himalayan salt or sea salt. Top with 1 large egg, fried (or scrambled) however you like. Get it while it's hot!

red pepper hummus toast

This healthy and satisfying spicy hummus is a bull's-eye for a midweek craving. Spread on toast and drizzle with a little olive oil. It also makes a great snack paired with carrot sticks, celery, cucumber slices, or baked corn tortilla chips.

Combine 1 can [15 oz/430 g] chickpeas, rinsed and drained well; ½ cup [120 g] chopped roasted red pepper, homemade (see page 99) or drained jarred; ¼ cup [55 g] tahini; ¼ cup [60 ml] fresh lemon juice; 2 Tbsp water; ½ tsp salt; ½ tsp cayenne pepper; and ½ tsp red pepper flakes in a blender or food processor and process to a completely smooth purée. Store in an airtight container in the refrigerator for up to a week.

cinnamon–almond butter toast

Making your own nut butters is way easier than you might think. This lightly spiced almond butter is amazing on warm toast. Top with a few fresh berries and it goes over the top!

Spread 2 cups [280 g] unsalted raw almonds on a baking sheet and bake in a 300°F [150°C] oven, until fragrant, about 15 minutes, stirring once or twice. Let cool, then combine in a high-powered blender with 3 Tbsp safflower oil. Process until the almonds are finely ground. Add 1 Tbsp raw honey, ½ tsp ground cinnamon, and ¼ tsp salt and process until smooth. Store in an airtight container in the refrigerator for up to 3 days.

creamy caprese toast

This toast is one of my favorite weekend treats. I don't want to get dramatic, but I believe it might be the mother ship of all toasts... I think it will float your boat, too.

Spread 1 Tbsp cream cheese on a thick slice of toasted Italian loaf. Top with a slice of fresh mozzarella cheese, a slice of ripe tomato, a few torn basil leaves, a drizzle of olive oil, and a few drops of balsamic vinegar.

goat cheese, fruit, and honey crostini

I love how balanced and delicious this toast combo is—the sharp tang of goat cheese with honey and fresh fruit. Use whatever fruit is in season.

Spread a generous amount of goat cheese on each crostini. Top with your favorite seasonal fruits and a drizzle of honey.

pink cream cheese toast

This garlicky, savory weekend spread is delicious, but the hot pink color takes it to another plane of delight. Add slices of avocado or cucumber, if you like. You're going to want to Instagram your breakfast—you may even want to paint its portrait!

In a food processor or blender, combine 8 oz [230 g] cream cheese, ½ cup [75 g] drained canned sliced beets, 2 tsp coarsely chopped garlic, and ½ tsp salt. Process to a completely smooth purée. Store in an airtight container in the refrigerator for up to 3 days.

whole-wheat english muffins

MAKES EIGHT SMALL MUFFINS

This great recipe delivers all the joy of fresh bread, whole-wheat goodness, and English muffin excitement—and is especially a boon if you have a hard time finding 100-percent whole-grain bread that you like at your local grocery store. Eat warm with vegan butter and a little honey, or some no-sugar-added jam or sliced fresh fruit. You can use these for any of the toast recipes in this book (pages 41–43), and also as the buns for the sandwiches and veggie burgers on pages 70–84.

¼ cup [60 ml] warm water

1 tsp pure maple syrup

2¼ tsp (1 envelope) active dry yeast

2¼ cups [315 g] white
  whole-wheat flour

¾ tsp salt

¾ cup [180 ml] almond milk

1 Tbsp coconut oil, melted

Whole-grain cornmeal (100 percent)
  for dusting (optional)

In a bowl, stir together the warm water and maple syrup until the syrup dissolves. Sprinkle the yeast over the top of the water and let sit for about 5 minutes. The yeast should begin to foam or bubble some; this lets you know that it's working. (If there's absolutely no sign of life after 10 to 15 minutes, discard the mixture and try a new envelope of yeast; check the date on the package to make sure it's not past its time.)

In a large bowl, whisk together the flour and salt and make a well in the center, then pour in the almond milk and coconut oil. Add the yeast mixture and stir until a rough dough ball forms. Cover the bowl with a clean kitchen towel and let the dough rest for 15 minutes.

continued . . .

Turn the dough out onto a lightly floured work surface and knead for about 5 minutes, until it begins to feel somewhat elastic. Place in a clean, lightly oiled bowl, cover with a clean kitchen towel, and let rise in warm, dry place for 1 hour, until doubled in bulk. The dough will look puffy and should deflate somewhat if poked or punched. (If my house is particularly cold, like it is during the winter months, I turn my oven on low while I prepare the dough. Then I turn it off, keeping the door shut, while I knead the dough. The residual warmth inside then provides the perfect haven for my dough while it's rising.)

Preheat the oven to 400°F [200°C]. Line a baking sheet with parchment paper or a silicone baking mat.

Divide the dough into 8 equal pieces and roll each into a ball, then flatten slightly into a disc about 1 inch [2.5 cm] thick. To really give these the look of an English muffin, dust your work surface with cornmeal and press the top and bottom of each muffin into it to lightly coat.

In a large, dry skillet over medium heat, cook the muffins a few at a time, turning once, until toasted, 4 to 5 minutes per side. Each side should look nicely browned, but if the muffins begin to burn, turn the heat down.

Transfer the toasted muffins to the prepared baking sheet and bake until lightly browned, 10 to 12 minutes. Cut one in half to check for doneness.

Let cool slightly, then split the muffins and eat warm. Or allow to cool completely and store in an airtight container at room temperature for up to 5 days. Split, rewarm, or toast when you are ready to eat them. You can also wrap them individually in wax paper and freeze them; once frozen, it's best to toast the muffins after thawing.

WEEKEND

Indulgent and leisurely weekend breakfasts are the coziest meals of the week. The following meals are geared for enjoying in your pajamas, possibly with a crossword puzzle. I know not every weekend breakfast can last for hours on end, but dare to dream! No matter how much time you have, let's indulge together a little; you deserve it after a week of carefully examining ingredient lists and working hard to incorporate more nutrition into your life. High five and pass the beignets (page 54)!

waffled french toast sandwiches

SERVES TWO

Here's one for all you lazy waffle-lovers out there. It's the weekend, so you may not feel like mixing together a batter but you still want those waffle ridges so you can fill them with butter or syrup—well then try this. It's a sandwich-waffle hybrid that you can change up the filling to whatever you have or whatever you love most: Nutella, other jellies or jams, sliced fresh fruit, cream cheese, hard cheeses, cooked veggie sausage patties, etc. Get creative, and enjoy the results of combining the pleasures of waffles, panini, and French toast.

4 slices French bread, or other rustic white bread you like

2 large eggs

3 Tbsp heavy cream or whole milk

½ tsp pure vanilla extract

¼ tsp ground cinnamon

2 slices Brie

¼ cup [75 g] apricot or fig jam

Powdered sugar and pure maple syrup for serving

Preheat a waffle iron. (If yours has settings, choose something in the middle.)

In a bowl large enough to fit one of the slices of bread, whisk together the eggs, cream, and vanilla until just combined. Sprinkle the cinnamon over the top and set aside.

Arrange the bread slices on a work surface. Place a slice of Brie on 2 of the slices. (I trim off the rind because I don't like the taste, but by all means keep it on if you're a fan.) Divide the jam between the other 2 slices, spreading it evenly.

Take up one of the Brie-topped bread slices in two hands and dip it carefully, bread-side down, into the egg mixture, letting the excess drip back into the bowl. Place the slice, battered-side down, on the hot waffle iron. Working quickly, dip a jam-topped slice of bread in the egg mixture the same way, then flip it jam-side down on top of the Brie and bread already in the waffle iron. Close the iron and cook until the bread is crispy and the cheese begins to melt, for 1½ to 2 minutes. Repeat to make the second sandwich.

Dust with powdered sugar and serve immediately, with a small serving dish of maple syrup for dipping.

halfway homemade beignets with blender hot chocolate

SERVES TWO OR THREE

This decadent dish definitely walks the line between breakfast and dessert. But I've always thought that donuts were a dessert masquerading as a breakfast. Not that I'm complaining! I choose a savory breakfast more often than not, so it's fun to really go for it when I opt for something sweet. A candy thermometer, also called a deep-frying thermometer, and a pair of heavy, spring-loaded tongs are helpful tools for this recipe (see Note, page 56).

1 can [7½ oz/215 g] store-bought buttermilk biscuits

2 to 4 cups [480 to 960 ml] canola or vegetable oil

¼ cup [30 g] powdered sugar

FOR THE HOT CHOCOLATE:

2 cups [480 ml] whole milk or half-and-half, or a mixture of the two

3 oz [85 g] dark or semisweet chocolate, chopped, or semisweet chocolate chips

Separate the biscuits and cut each biscuit into 4 equal pieces.

Pour oil into a wide, heavy-bottomed pot to a depth that will allow the biscuit pieces to float. Clip a candy or deep-frying thermometer to the side of the pot and heat the oil to 350°F [180°C].

When the oil is hot, add a few pieces of biscuit at a time, being careful to not crowd the pot. After 20 to 30 seconds, using tongs, flip each beignet and cook for another 20 to 30 seconds, until each piece is golden brown on all sides. Transfer to a plate lined with paper towels to soak up the excess oil.

continued . . .

A Beautiful Mess

When all the beignets are fried, use a fine-mesh sieve or sifter to dust them with powdered sugar. Make sure you coat each one pretty heavily. (This is the number-one thing I learned when I visited Café du Monde in New Orleans—go nuts with the powdered sugar. That's how the beignet pros do it.)

Cover the beignets to keep warm while you quickly pull together the hot chocolate: Heat the milk over medium-high heat until very hot but not boiling. Meanwhile, put the chocolate in a blender. When the milk is quite hot, carefully pour it into the blender. Cover the blender with its lid and place a folded kitchen towel over the top, just in case any hot liquid escapes from around the lid. (Be careful not to burn your hand if you are holding the top.) Blend until the chocolate has melted and incorporated into the milk and it's gotten a bit frothy, 30 to 45 seconds.

Pour the hot chocolate into mugs and serve with the beignets. For the full experience, try dipping the beignets in the hot chocolate. Now that's a weekend.

Note: If you don't own one or both of these kitchen champs, I recommend investing—and neither is very expensive. You'll find yourself reaching for the tongs all the time, and the high-register thermometer is useful for any deep-frying as well as making syrups and candies from caramel to peanut brittle to homemade marshmallows.

breakfast stuffing

SERVES THREE AS A MAIN OR UP TO SIX AS A SIDE

This recipe has the added bonus of making your whole kitchen smell like Thanksgiving. With its simple, comforting ingredients, I think this version makes a great weekend breakfast option any time of year—but especially on chilly mornings when something warm is called for. Choose between celery or apple to add crunch; the apple adds a little sweetness as well. This main-dish stuffing is also a great side dish to take to a brunch potluck.

Note, you really want your cubed bread quite dry so it will soak up more moisture. I will often cube my bread the night before and leave it out, uncovered, before throwing this together in the morning if I don't think my bread is sufficiently dry already. If you have some stale bread lying around then this or French toast is the way to use it up.

3 Tbsp unsalted butter, plus more for greasing

⅓ red onion, chopped (about ⅔ cup/90 g)

1 celery stalk or ½ tart apple such as Granny Smith, chopped

3 cloves garlic, minced

4 cups [240 g] dry rustic white bread cubes (I love using a French loaf here; about half an average loaf, day old, is usually just about right)

1 tsp chopped fresh sage

1 tsp chopped fresh thyme

1 tsp chopped fresh rosemary

⅔ cup [160 ml] vegetable stock, homemade or good-quality low-sodium store-bought

4 large eggs

Salt and freshly ground pepper

1 Tbsp heavy cream or whole milk

Smoky Coconut Flakes (page 129) for garnish (optional)

continued . . .

A Beautiful Mess

Preheat the oven to 375°F [190°C].

In a skillet, melt 2 Tbsp of the butter over medium heat. Add the onion and celery and cook, stirring occasionally, until the onion begins to soften and appear translucent, 3 to 4 minutes. Add the garlic and cook for 1 more minute. Remove from the heat.

In a large bowl, combine the bread cubes, onion mixture, and herbs. In a small bowl, combine the vegetable stock and 1 of the eggs and beat lightly until just blended. Pour the vegetable stock mixture over bread cube mixture and toss so that everything is well coated and combined.

Spoon the stuffing into a buttered pie pan and spread in an even layer. Using the back of a large spoon, gently press 3 indentations into the top, spacing them evenly. These will hold (and act as a mold for) the remaining 3 eggs. Sprinkle generously with salt and pepper.

Bake the stuffing for 25 minutes. Remove from the oven and carefully crack an egg into each of the indentations you created earlier. (I crack each egg into a small bowl before adding to the stuffing, in case I have any stray eggshell that needs to get picked out first. But if you feel super-confident in your egg cracking skills, you can add them directly to the dish.) Top each egg with a little cream or whole milk, so the tops don't dry out while baking.

Bake until the whites look set but the yolks will likely still be nice and runny, 8 or 9 minutes longer. Use the large spoon to scoop onto individual plates or into bowls, cutting each serving so it includes an egg, unless serving as a side option. Serve immediately, with a little crumbled smoky coconut over the top, if you like.

easy bourbon and peach hand pies

MAKES EIGHT HAND PIES; SERVES FOUR

These are such a fun and easy weekend treat. Unless I am taking these over to a friend's house or we have guests that weekend, we don't usually eat all 8 of these in one sitting. This works out great, as it means I can warm one up later that afternoon with a second cup of coffee, if that's what the day allows for. I love the flaky crust paired with a sweet-and-spicy peach filling that you can throw together in just minutes. We use a little bourbon to add a little more flavor, but if you don't have, or don't like, bourbon, substitute vanilla extract. But, who doesn't like bourbon? I mean, really.

2 sheets puff pastry, each 10 by 15 inches (25 by 38 cm)
3 ripe peaches
¼ cup [45 g] firmly packed brown sugar
1 tsp bourbon
⅛ tsp ground cinnamon
1 large egg (optional)

FOR THE GLAZE:
½ cup [60 g] powdered sugar
3 tsp whole milk, heavy cream, or water

Preheat the oven to 400°F [200°C].

Thaw the puff pastry sheets according to the package directions.

Meanwhile, peel and pit the peaches and cut into very small cubes. Put the peaches in a bowl and add the brown sugar, bourbon, and cinnamon. Stir gently with a large spoon to coat all the pieces. At first the mixture may seem too dry, but the peach pieces will begin to release moisture, so be sure your puff pastry is thawed and ready to go by the time you have everything stirred together.

continued . . .

A Beautiful Mess

Cut each puff pastry sheet into 8 same-sized triangles. Place a tablespoon or so of the peach mixture in the center of one triangle, then place another triangle on top. Use the tines of a fork to press the edges together, and then poke a few holes in the top, using the tips of the tines. Repeat to assemble the remaining hand pies, arranging them on a baking sheet lined with parchment paper or a silicone baking mat as you work.

In a small bowl, beat the egg well with a fork. Using a pastry brush, lightly brush the tops of the hand pies with the egg wash. This is optional, but it will give your hand pies a glossy, golden tone and an oh-so-pastry-shop-professional look.

Bake until the pastry is very puffy and deep golden brown, 18 to 20 minutes. Transfer to a wire cooling rack and let cool.

To make the glaze, in a small bowl, whisk together the powdered sugar and milk. When the hand pies have cooled for a few minutes, drizzle the glaze over the top of each. Serve warm. Store for up to 2 days in an airtight container; rewarm gently in the microwave or oven before serving.

baked eggs in spicy tomato sauce

SERVES ONE OR TWO

I LOVE this dish. It's got a little of everything I like: spice, cheese, runny egg yolks, and crusty, warm bread. You also can easily change it up to be suitable for weekday eating; just omit the cheese and swap out the buttery baguette for whole-wheat toast. It's still totally delicious that way, but I must admit, I like the weekend version best, which is why we include it in this section. This saucy, cheesy comfort food also makes a great breakfast-for-dinner option when paired with a glass of red wine and a rom com. (No, the rom com is not optional.)

2 to 3 Tbsp unsalted butter

2 tsp olive oil

2 Tbsp chopped onion

3 cloves garlic, minced

1 can (14½ oz/415 g) whole plum tomatoes

1 Tbsp harissa (see Note, page 65)

¼ tsp red pepper flakes

2 large eggs

½ tsp heavy cream or whole milk

2 Tbsp crumbled feta cheese

2 big leaves fresh basil, chopped

2 to 4 slices baguette, toasted

Preheat the oven to 375°F [190°C].

In an 8-in [20-cm] cast-iron skillet or other oven-safe pan, melt ½ Tbsp of the butter and warm with the olive oil over medium heat. Add the onion and sauté until soft, about 3 minutes. Add the garlic and cook for 1 minute longer.

Meanwhile, drain the tomatoes. (They don't have to be perfectly drained, just the majority of the juices.) Add the tomatoes and harissa to a blender or food processor and process to a smooth or coarse purée. (I like something in the middle.)

Add the tomato mixture and red pepper flakes to the skillet and continue to cook over medium heat until some of the liquid has reduced, 6 to 8 minutes. Spread in an even layer in the pan.

continued . . .

One at a time, crack the eggs onto the surface of sauce, putting a few inches between them. (I like to crack the eggs one by one into a small bowl first, so I can catch any shell pieces that might come off before adding them to my sauce. If you feel super-confident in your egg-cracking skills, you can add them directly to the pan.) Drizzle ¼ tsp cream over each yolk to keep them from drying out while baking.

Transfer to the oven and bake for 6 minutes. Check the dish; remove it from the oven if you need to for a good look, because you want this dish to finish just right. My goal is to catch it at the perfect point when the whites are set but the yolks are still runny; this usually happens around the 7 minute mark, but since eggs cook so quickly and every oven is a little different (and even the same oven is different on different days), it's best to just keep a sharp eye on it at the moment of truth. You can cook for up to 9 minutes, if you prefer yolks that are mostly set (but I'd be sorry if you did; that warm runny yolk is delicious spilling into the mix). Keep in mind too that the eggs will continue to cook a little after they are removed from the oven.

Sprinkle the feta and basil over the top of the baked eggs. Lightly butter the baguette toasts with the remaining butter. As soon as the eggs and sauce are cool enough to eat, spoon on individual plates or bowls, or enjoy straight out of the pan.

Note: A paste that is North African in origin, harissa is most often a blend of various hot chiles and peppers, along with garlic, olive oil (making it a great source of anti-inflammatory fats), and spices. It's an incredibly versatile and flavorful ingredient: use it as a rub, add it to sauces, or try it as a condiment with any meal that needs a jolt of smoky heat. Most gourmet and specialty grocery stores have it stocked nowadays, but it can also be found at your local Middle Eastern market or online.

me

als

WEEKDAY

There is not enough space in this book to show you how much variety and delicious choice you really have when it comes to putting together a healthy weekday meal. I hope you'll see that although we cut a few fun things out of our diet during the week, we still have plenty of room for all sorts of tasty stuff.

Pasta and pizza are two of my favorite food categories, so if you just got excited reading the words "Pasta and Pizza," then we are kindred spirits. There are so many whole-grain and other alternatives available when it comes to these venerated genres—and man oh man, am I glad there are!

The following are some of my very favorite meals, sauces, and sides—things that I make over and over again. Please feel free to adapt these after you've given them a first try and to make them your own! Nothing would make me happier. Here's to a happy and healthy week!

from the nutritionists

We hope you'll be so blown away by these weekday meal recipes you won't mind packing leftovers. When it comes to weekday meals, variety and color are key. All of the recipes found in this section are simply bursting with nutrients, vitamins, minerals, fiber, and antioxidants. You will notice that most of the dishes are plant-based and incorporate whole, organic ingredients. The concept here is not ground-breaking: a plant-based diet biologically makes sense. It's how our ancestors thrived and what we now really should be focusing more of our diet on. We recommend filling at least half of your plate with fresh fruits and vegetables. Balance out the remaining surface with lean protein, whole grains, and healthy fats. Not an herbivore? Don't panic. Plant-based doesn't just mean vegetables; we're talking whole grains, legumes, seeds, fresh fruits. The idea is less junk, more of the fresh stuff.

Shop as local as possible. Not only are you supporting your community and local businesses, but the less distance your food has to travel the more likely it is to yield a fresh nutritious product. We can't say enough about farmers' markets, CSAs, community gardens, farm stands, and the positive effects they have on your health, wallet, and community.

Some of our favorite recipes in this section are the sauces and toppings. It's incredible how a simple condiment can transform a dish. When buying dressings or sauces in grocery stores, it can be easy to grab something that looks healthy, only to read the label and discover it's filled with additives you can't pronounce. We recommend preparing your own dressings and sauces as much as possible to avoid nasty ingredients, which are often inexpensive flavor additives that are used to save money, maintain shelf stability, enhance flavor, and make us crave the product.

On a final note, as dietitians we believe meat and fish can be included in a healthy diet, so if you'd like to add meat to these dishes, feel free! Whether fresh cuts of beef, pork chops, salmon, tuna, roasted turkey, or venison, we suggest you select fresh meat sources to avoid salt, nitrates, nitrites, and other additives. If you are able, source your meat from a local farmer who can tell you what the animal was fed, where it was raised, and that it was treated kindly and ethically. Another great option is to use a local butcher who puts his or her faith into the raising, butchering, and distribution of their meat product.

savory dill and apple salad sandwich

SERVES ONE

I put together this refreshing combo all the time for myself as a quick workday lunch. It's fast, crunchy, savory, and really delicious. If I'm really hungry I eat this entire serving between two toasted slices of whole grain bread. If I'm feeling less hungry or I'm eating this along with something else (like carrot sticks and hummus—yum!), then I'll just eat half of this over one piece of toast as a kind of open-faced sandwich. This works well too if you are feeding two people at once.

½ crisp apple such as Granny Smith, cored and cubed

¼ cup [30 g] slivered almonds

1 Tbsp chopped red onion

1 Tbsp chopped fresh dill

1 Tbsp fresh lemon juice

1 heaping Tbsp mayonnaise, store-bought (no sugar added) or homemade (page 125)

½ tsp celery seed

1 tsp yellow mustard (no sugar added)

Salt and freshly ground pepper

2 slices whole-grain bread, toasted if you like

Lettuce leaves and sliced cucumbers for topping

In a bowl, combine the apple, almonds, onion, dill, lemon juice, mayo, celery seed, and mustard and stir to combine and coat everything well. Season with salt and pepper.

Pile the salad on one of the slices of bread, arrange lettuce leaves and cuke slices on top, and close the sandwich up with the second bread slice. Press gently to help everything hold together. Cut in half and serve immediately or no more than a few hours after it's assembled.

curried deviled egg sandwich

SERVES ONE

This is another weekday lunch favorite of mine; it only takes minutes to make if you have already hard-boiled your eggs. Here's my dirty little secret: in a pinch, I buy eggs already hard-boiled from a grocery store where I know they'll be good-quality and fresh. In addition to sandwiches, I can slice them up and add them to a salad; and of course a hard-boiled egg with a little salt and pepper is always a great weekday snack, as well.

2 hard-boiled eggs (see Note, page 74), peeled

1 Tbsp mayonnaise, store-bought (no sugar added) or homemade (page 125)

1 tsp yellow mustard

½ tsp toasted curry powder (see Note)

¼ tsp toasted caraway seeds

Salt and freshly ground pepper

2 slices whole-wheat bread, toasted

Spinach or lettuce leaves for topping

Cut the hard-boiled eggs into small cubes and place in a small bowl. Add the mayo, mustard, curry powder, and caraway seeds. Stir gently to combine and coat everything well. Season with salt and pepper.

Spread the salad on one piece of the toasted bread slices. Top with spinach or lettuce leaves, if you like (it's delicious all on its own, too). Close the sandwich up with the second bread slice. Press gently to help everything hold together. Cut in half and serve immediately.

Note: Toasting spices briefly brings out the aromas and deepens the flavor. Just heat a small, dry skillet over medium-low heat. Add the spice powder (or whole spice) and toast, stirring or swirling the pan constantly to prevent burning and to help cook it evenly, until fragrant, 2 to 3 minutes. Pour into a small bowl immediately and let cool.

continued . . .

Note: Making hard-boiled eggs is very easy, but there are a few seemingly minor techniques that can make it completely foolproof (my favorite kitchen term). Place the eggs in a small to medium pot and fill with enough water to cover the eggs. Bring the water to a rolling boil over high heat. Then turn off the heat, cover, and allow the eggs to cook in the hot water for 5 to 12 minutes, depending on how done you like your yolks (5 to 6 minutes for soft, 7 to 8 minutes for medium-soft, and 10 to 12 minutes for hard—which is what I usually aim for with hard-boiled eggs). Fill a bowl with ice and water. Using a slotted spoon, transfer the eggs to this ice bath, to stop the cooking process. After a minute or two the eggs will be cool enough to handle. Gently crack the shells on a hard surface. Then peel the egg under a trickle of cool, running water, to help remove the peel without creating craters in your egg white. Store any eggs you don't plan to use right away in an airtight container in the refrigerator for up to 5 days.

pulled squash sandwiches with grilled onion and pineapple

SERVES FOUR

This sandwich is based on a Midwest favorite, pulled pork sandwiches. Here we cook the spaghetti squash so the "meat" becomes soft enough to be easily pulled away in ribbons. Then we combine these delicious strands with BBQ sauce and grilled pineapple for a tangy and lightly sweet sandwich. Serve alongside coleslaw to add even more crunch (and vegetables). Yum!

1 spaghetti squash, about 6 oz [170 g]

2 tsp olive oil

Salt and freshly ground pepper

½ red onion, thickly sliced

4 big slices fresh pineapple

¾ cup [195 g] Homemade BBQ Sauce (page 126)

8 slices whole-wheat bread or 4 whole-wheat burger buns, toasted if you like

Lettuce or shredded cabbage for topping (optional)

Preheat the oven to 375°F [190°C].

Using a large chef's knife, cut the spaghetti squash in half. Using a large spoon, scoop out the seeds and membranes from each half. Brush 1 tsp of the olive oil over the insides and season with a little salt and pepper. Place in a baking pan, cut-side up. Bake until very tender when pierced with a fork or thin-bladed knife, 50 to 60 minutes. Remove from the oven and let cool. When cool enough to handle, use a fork to shred, or pull, the flesh out of the shells. It should come away easily in long strands. Spread the pulled squash on a baking sheet or a couple of large plates lined with paper towels to remove excess moisture. (You want to remove as much moisture as you can, so don't pile the squash on top of itself for this step; give yourself enough room to spread it out over the paper towels.)

continued . . .

Lightly oil a grill pan with the remaining 1 tsp olive oil and heat over medium-high heat. Arrange the onion and pineapple slices in the pan. Do not crowd the pan (you may need to work in two batches). Cook, turning once, until the pineapple and onion soften and are nicely grill-marked, 2 to 3 minutes per side. Transfer to a plate as each piece is finished.

In a large bowl, stir together the squash and BBQ sauce. (If the squash has gotten cold, warm it up in the microwave for a few seconds.) Arrange 4 of the bread slices on your work surface. Distribute the pulled BBQ squash evenly among them. Top each with one-fourth of the grilled onions and pineapple. Add a lettuce leaf or two if you want a little more crunch. Close the sandwiches up with the remaining bread slices. Press gently to help everything hold together. Cut in half and serve warm.

Note: If you aren't going to make a whole batch of 4 sandwiches, then only make enough grilled onion and pineapple for how many you are planning. You can store the BBQ pulled squash in an airtight container in the refrigerator for up to 2 days. Rewarm gently for the next round.

barbecue
sweet potato burgers

SERVES FOUR TO SIX

I grew up eating hamburgers, being from southern Missouri with a cattle farmer for a grandfather (miss you Papa!). So when I discover a veggie burger that hits the spot, I am both excited and grateful. What I love most about homemade veggie burgers is how you can easily make quite a few at once and freeze them. This can make weekday lunches or I-worked-late-and-don't-feel-like-cooking dinners a breeze without derailing you from your healthy-eating goal.

You can serve these wrapped in big lettuce leaves; with whole-wheat English muffins for buns (see ours on page 46); or even with roasted portobello mushrooms as bun alternatives. I like to stir together a little hot sauce and homemade mayo (page 125) to spread on top, or you could garnish with more BBQ sauce. Your options are endless here!

1 large sweet potato,
   about 15 oz [430 g]

2 tsp olive oil

Salt and freshly ground pepper

4 cloves garlic, minced

1 cup [90 g] textured vegetable
   protein (TVP) (see Note, page 84)

2 Tbsp soy sauce

2 Tbsp Homemade BBQ Sauce (page 126)

1 large egg

About 1 cup [140 g] white
   whole-wheat flour

2 Tbsp olive oil

Whole-grain buns or lettuce
   leaves for serving (see recipe
   introduction)

Preheat the oven to 375°F [190°C]. Line a baking sheet with parchment paper or a silicone baking mat.

Peel and cube the potato and pile it on the prepared baking sheet. Drizzle with the olive oil and season with salt and pepper. Toss to mix and coat well, then spread the cubes in a single layer on the baking sheet. Bake until the potatoes are tender enough to cut easily with the side of a fork, 25 to 35 minutes. Remove from the oven and let cool. When the potato is cooled, transfer to a large bowl and mash with the garlic. Set aside.

continued . . .

In a microwave-safe bowl, stir together the TVP, soy sauce, and BBQ sauce. Microwave on high until just warm, 10 to 20 seconds. (If you hate microwaves or don't own one, you can do this step on the stovetop in a small saucepan instead. The goal is to warm the liquids so that they will soften the TVP.)

Add the TVP mixture to the bowl with the mashed sweet potato. Add the egg and ½ cup [70 g] of the flour. Stir until well blended. The mixture should hold together and form a ball easily. If it feels too wet and sticky, mix in more flour in small increments until the consistency is right.

Divide the burger mixture into 4 to 6 equal portions. Using your clean hands, form each portion into a burger patty. Put the remaining flour on a plate or in a shallow bowl. Lightly dip each patty in the flour on both sides. Wrap the patties individually in plastic wrap and refrigerate for at least 30 minutes and up to 3 days, or freeze to save for longer periods. (If you freeze the burgers, thaw gently in the fridge before cooking.)

To cook the burgers, in a large skillet, heat the oil over medium heat. Add the burgers, being careful not to crowd the pan, and pan-fry, turning once, until crispy and browned, 4 to 5 minutes on each side. Tuck into buns and serve right away.

chipotle-black bean burgers

SERVES FOUR

Now we're talking! This is my very favorite "classic" veggie burger recipe. Black beans add not just nutrition but also the expected and appealing rich dark color to these burger patties; and I just love the added kick the chipotle pepper brings. These are unassuming but totally delicious, and very easy to make too. I think you're going to fall for them as much as I have. I like to top mine with lettuce and either mustard or Homemade BBQ Sauce (page 126), but you can add any of your favorite Weekday burger toppings.

¼ cup [60 ml] water

1 Tbsp soy sauce

½ cup [45 g] textured vegetable protein (TVP) (see Note, page 84)

1 can (15 oz/430 g) black beans, rinsed and drained

1 to 2 chipotle peppers in adobo sauce

1 tsp onion powder

1 tsp garlic powder

½ tsp salt

⅓ cup [45 g] white whole-wheat flour

2 Tbsp olive oil

Whole-grain buns or lettuce leaves for serving (see recipe introduction)

In a medium microwave-safe bowl, stir together the water, soy sauce, and TVP. Microwave on high until warm, 10 to 20 seconds. (If you hate microwaves, you can do this step in a small saucepan on the stove top.) Remove from the microwave and stir so the TVP softens a little. Set aside.

In a food processor, combine half of the black beans, the chipotle pepper(s) to taste, the onion powder, garlic powder, and salt. Process to a uniform paste. (It doesn't have to be a perfectly smooth texture, but you do want to make sure the chipotle is well distributed throughout.)

Add the bean paste to the bowl with the TVP mixture. Add the remaining black beans and the flour. Stir until just blended. Cover and refrigerate for 20 minutes.

continued . . .

Divide the burger mixture into 4 equal portions. Using your clean hands, form each portion into a burger patty. Wrap the patties individually in plastic wrap and refrigerate for at least 30 minutes and up to 3 days, or freeze to save for longer periods. (If you freeze the burgers, thaw gently in the fridge before cooking.)

To cook the burgers, in a large skillet, heat the oil over medium heat. Add the burgers, being careful not to crowd the pan, and pan-fry, turning once, until each side is browned and slightly crispy, 4 to 5 minutes per side. Press your finger on each patty to make sure it feels heated throughout. Tuck into buns and serve right away.

Note: Made from soy flour (a byproduct of soybean oil) and formed into various shapes (any shape!), Textured Vegetable Protein (TVP) is incredibly easy to use and quick to cook. Use it instead of meat to make your meal vegetarian or substitute it for half the meat to cut cost. You can find TVP in most major natural food stores (Whole Foods, for example) or online. It is sold in various "cuts," including chucks, flakes, or strips to suit any need. Most TVP products have to be reconstituted in boiling water; see the package for cooking times.

baked falafel with creamy cucumber slaw

SERVES FOUR

This falafel recipe can easily be shaped into 4 burger-sized patties or 8 mini slider patties. More often than not I will shape them into the smaller, slider-size patties and after cooking I'll top with chopped cucumber and drizzle the dressing over everything. This way we keep all the delicious flavors that come with falafel but the meal is overall a bit lighter for our weekday goal.

1 can [15 oz/430 g] chickpeas, rinsed and drained
3 Tbsp chopped red onion
3 cloves garlic, chopped
2 Tbsp chopped fresh parsley
2 Tbsp chopped fresh cilantro
1 tsp salt
1 tsp arrowroot powder (see Note, page 35)
¼ cup [35 g] white whole-wheat flour, plus more for dusting
Vegetable or olive oil for greasing

FOR THE DRESSING:
3 Tbsp tahini
1 clove garlic, minced
2 Tbsp fresh lemon juice
1 Tbsp honey or pure maple syrup
1 Tbsp olive oil
Salt and freshly ground pepper
2 to 3 Tbsp water, or as needed

1 large cucumber, peeled, seeded, and diced
Za'atar for garnish (optional)

In a food processor or blender, combine the chickpeas, onion, garlic, parsley, cilantro, and salt. Process until smooth and no large lumps remain.

Transfer the chickpea mixture to a bowl and stir in the arrowroot and flour until thoroughly blended. Cover the bowl with plastic wrap and refrigerate for 30 minutes, or freeze for 10 minutes.

Preheat the oven to 350°F [180°C]. Lightly oil a baking sheet.

Remove the falafel mixture from the fridge. Divide the mixture into either 4 equal portions for hamburger-sized patties or 8 for slider-sized patties. Lightly flour your clean hands and roll each portion into a ball, then flatten into a disc. (If you are not planning to cook all the patties, wrap any extras individually in plastic wrap and refrigerate for up to 3 days, or freeze until you need them. If you freeze the patties, thaw gently in the fridge before cooking.)

continued . . .

To bake, arrange the patties on the prepared baking sheet and bake for 10 minutes. Remove the pan from the oven and, using a spatula, turn the patties. Return to the oven and continue baking until crisp on both sides, 10 to 12 minutes longer.

Meanwhile, make the dressing: In a glass measuring cup, stir together the tahini, garlic, lemon juice, honey, and olive oil. Taste and adjust the seasoning with salt and pepper. Thin the sauce with water until easily pourable, if necessary.

When the falafel is done, divide the patties among individual plates. Top with the cucumber, then drizzle the sauce over everything. Sprinkle generously with za'atar, if using. Serve warm.

mushroom ragù

SERVES TWO

Lots of vegetables come together in this thick and hearty tomato sauce. Served over whole-wheat or gluten-free (such as quinoa or brown rice) spaghetti or fettuccini, meaty non-meat mushroom ragù is comfort food at its ultimate. For equally satisfying but low-carb alternatives, serve atop shredded spaghetti squash (see page 76) or lightly sautéed spiralized zucchini noodles (see page 91).

1 Tbsp olive oil

¼ cup [35 g] finely chopped red onion

1 celery stalk, finely chopped

1 carrot, peeled and finely chopped

8 oz [230 g] cremini (baby bella) mushrooms, brushed clean

3 cloves garlic

¼ cup [23 g] textured vegetable protein (TVP) (see Note, page 84)

¼ tsp ground cumin

¼ tsp cayenne pepper

3 tsp salt

½ tsp freshly ground black pepper

1 can [28 oz/800 g] whole plum tomatoes

½ lb [230 g] whole-wheat or gluten-free spaghetti or fettuccini (see recipe introduction)

1 Tbsp chopped fresh parsley

Non-Dairy Parmesan (page 128) for sprinkling

In a large saucepan, heat the olive oil over medium heat. Add the onion, celery, and carrot and cook until softened, 2 to 3 minutes, stirring every so often with a big wooden spoon. Meanwhile, chop up the mushrooms and mince the garlic.

When the aromatics are softened, add the garlic to the pan and cook for 1 minute longer. (If any of the ingredients appear to be burning at any point, turn the heat down. If things seem to be sticking to the pan, add a little more oil.)

Add the mushrooms and cook for a minute or two, stirring, until they begin to release moisture. Scatter in the TVP and season everything with the cumin, cayenne, ½ tsp of the salt, and the black pepper. Stir to mix well and reduce the heat to medium-low.

Stir 2 tsp salt into a pot of water and bring to a boil.

continued . . .

In a blender or food processor, process the tomatoes with their juices to a nice saucy consistency, just a few seconds (they don't have to be completely smooth), then add to the pan. Stir in the remaining ½ tsp salt and continue to cook over medium-low heat, stirring, until the sauce begins to reduce and thicken, 12 to 15 minutes.

Meanwhile, add the pasta to the boiling water and cook until al dente according to the package directions.

When the sauce is thick enough so that you can run a wooden spoon through it and it leaves a trail before the sauce begins to seep back into place, remove from the heat.

To serve, drain the pasta well and divide among individual plates or pasta bowls. Spoon over the ragù generously. Top each portion with the parsley and Parmesan and serve immediately.

A Beautiful Mess

zoodles and noodles teriyaki stir-fry

SERVES TWO

I love combining what we like to call "zoodles"—zucchini that's been spiralized into a noodle shape—with whole-wheat spaghetti noodles; I think the two balance each other's textures beautifully. The zucchini noodles soften when cooked, while the whole-wheat noodles offer more body than their white-flour cousins. At the same time, by mixing the two, you reduce the overall carbs and raise the nutrient count on your plate.

Feel free to change up the vegetables in this stir-fry. I use bell peppers most often, but other great options include broccoli, mushrooms, Brussels sprouts, and asparagus. For additional protein, add some chopped baked tofu.

FOR THE TERIYAKI SAUCE:

¼ cup [60 ml] soy sauce

2 Tbsp Homemade BBQ Sauce (page 126)

1 Tbsp rice vinegar

1 Tbsp honey or pure maple syrup

2 tsp sesame oil

2 cloves garlic, minced

¼ tsp ground ginger

⅛ tsp red pepper flakes

4 oz [115 g] whole-wheat spaghetti

2 tsp olive oil

1 red bell pepper, seeded and thinly sliced

1 small zucchini, spiralized or cut into thin matchsticks

2 Tbsp chopped cashew nuts, preferably raw

1 Tbsp chopped green onion

continued . . .

Bring a pot of generously salted water to a boil.

To make the Teriyaki Sauce, in a small saucepan, combine the soy sauce, BBQ sauce, vinegar, honey, sesame oil, garlic, ginger, and red pepper flakes and stir to mix well. Bring to a boil and cook for 2 minutes, stirring often. Remove from the heat and set aside.

Meanwhile, add the spaghetti to the boiling water and cook until al dente according to the package directions. Drain well and set aside.

When the sauce and the spaghetti are ready, in a large saucepan or skillet, heat the olive oil over high heat. Add the bell pepper and cook, stirring often, until starting to soften, about 1 minute. Add the zucchini noodles and cooked and drained pasta. Pour the sauce over everything and stir-fry, tossing to mix and coat well, until the sauce thickens up a little, 2 to 3 minutes.

To serve, divide the stir-fry between 2 plates. Sprinkle the cashews and green onions on top and serve immediately.

Note: If you find this is a meal you end up making often feel free to double the sauce recipe and make enough for another meal later. You can store the unused sauce in a sealed container in the refrigerator for up to two weeks.

A Beautiful Mess

whole-wheat pizza crust + topping ideas

SERVES TWO OR THREE

It's a good thing the number-one rule in Weekday Weekend is to eat a variety of foods. Otherwise I would eat this pizza crust all the time. I even use this same recipe on the weekends for cheesy pizzas; it's just that good. Below I give you a few ideas for things you can top your pizza crust with but feel free to change it up based on what vegetables you may have left over in your refrigerator or what is in season where you live. Pizza toppings are a great place to try new combinations—because you really can't go wrong. Everything tastes delicious on a pizza.

FOR THE DOUGH:

¾ cup [180 ml] warm water

1 tsp pure maple syrup

2¼ tsp (1 envelope) active dry yeast

1 cup plus 2 Tbsp [160 g] white whole-wheat flour

1 tsp salt

¼ cup [60 ml] olive oil, plus more for greasing

Whole-grain cornmeal or more flour for dusting

FOR THE SAUCE (A FEW IDEAS, OR USE YOUR OWN WEEKDAY-FRIENDLY FAVORITES):

Store-bought (no sugar added) tomato sauce

BBQ sauce, homemade (page 126) or store-bought (no sugar added)

Non-Dairy Basil Pesto (page 127)

IDEAS FOR TOPPINGS:

A bunch of sautéed veggies— I love caramelized onions, garlic, bell peppers, pineapple, and jalapeño best.

Non-Dairy Parmesan (page 128)

Smoky Coconut Flakes (especially yummy with BBQ pizza; page 129)

In a small bowl, stir together the warm water and maple syrup until the syrup dissolves. Sprinkle the yeast over the top and let stand for 5 minutes.

continued . . .

In a large bowl, whisk together the flour and salt. Make a well in the center and pour in the ¼ cup [60 ml] olive oil and the yeast mixture. Stir until a rough dough ball forms. (The dough will be quite wet, but it should hold together loosely.) Let rest for 10 minutes.

Turn the dough out onto a lightly floured work surface and knead for 2 to 3 minutes. Pat into a round, place in a clean, lightly oiled bowl, cover with a clean dish towel, and let rise for 1 hour, until doubled in bulk. It should double or nearly double in size during this time.

Preheat the oven to 400°F [200°C]. Oil a large baking sheet. If using a stone no need to add oil. Dust lightly with cornmeal or additional whole-wheat flour to keep the crust from sticking.

Turn out the dough onto a clean, lightly floured work surface and roll out into a 15-in [38-cm] round. Transfer to the prepared baking sheet. Bake for 5 minutes—the crust will slightly puff and just begin to brown on the edges—then remove from the oven and add your choice of sauce and toppings (see recipe introduction). Return to the oven and bake until the crust is golden, the sauce is bubbling, the toppings are tender, 7 to 10 minutes longer. Remove from the oven and let cool briefly, then cut into wedges and serve hot.

tomato and roasted red pepper soup

SERVES TWO OR THREE

There are days when it feels like everything has gone wrong. Maybe I didn't sleep well the night before, I missed a deadline at work, and I arrive home to see our dog has torn up yet another pair of shoes. It's a far cry from tragedy, but I find that it's days like this that can really throw me off of my routines and goals, like completing the Weekday Weekend challenge. It's because I just want to be comforted. The good news: that's exactly what this soup is. It's a hearty, slightly spicy, super flavorful bowl of comfort that won't derail your weekday goal. Make this soup!

2 Tbsp olive oil

½ white onion, chopped

3 cloves garlic, minced

1 can [15 oz/430 g] diced tomatoes, with juices

2 roasted red peppers, homemade (see Note, page 99) or drained jarred

1 Tbsp harissa (see Note, page 65)

Salt and freshly ground pepper

Whole-wheat bread cubes, toasted, for serving

In a soup pot, heat 1 tablespoon of the olive oil over medium heat. Add the onion and cook, stirring often, until transparent and lightly golden, about 5 minutes. Add the garlic and cook for 1 minute longer. Add the tomatoes and their juices and the roasted red peppers and stir well. Cook over medium-low heat for about 5 minutes longer, stirring occasionally, to allow the flavors to blend.

Remove the soup from the heat. Using an immersion blender directly in the pot, or in a blender, process the soup to a smooth purée. (If using a blender, work carefully in batches to make sure you do not to burn yourself with the hot liquid.)

continued . . .

Return the soup to the pot, if you used a blender. Stir well, add the harissa, and cook for a few minutes. Taste and adjust the seasoning with salt and pepper. Ladle into bowls, top with the whole-wheat croutons, and serve hot.

Note: You can find roasted red peppers in a jar, which makes this an even easier meal to prepare when you're short on time. But if you can't find them, it's easy to roast your own, which will also bring fresh flavor to the dish: Preheat the broiler. Remove the stems, ribs, and seeds from 2 large red bell peppers. Cut each pepper in fourths. Grease a baking sheet with olive oil and place the peppers on the pan, cut-side down. Broil until the skins are wrinkled all over and charred in spots, 6 to 8 minutes. (Every broiler is a little different, so keep a close eye on the peppers to avoid burning.) Transfer the peppers to a paper bag, seal, and let steam for 5 to 10 minutes. When they are just cool enough to handle, remove from the bags and peel off the skins. Use as directed in any recipe.

chipotle-sweet potato soup

SERVES TWO OR THREE

This is one of those recipes that I've been making for years and it never gets old. The sweetness from the potatoes alongside the heat from the pepper make for a super flavorful and interesting combination. This soup is already quite substantial due to the heartiness of the potato, but if you'd like to serve alongside some toasted whole-wheat bread for dipping purposes I won't stop you. This soup makes a great lunch the next day as well.

1 Tbsp olive oil

½ yellow onion, chopped

2 cloves garlic, minced

1 large sweet potato, about 15 oz [430 g], peeled and cubed

½ to 1 chipotle pepper in adobo sauce (see Note)

2 cups [480 ml] vegetable stock, homemade or good-quality low-sodium store-bought

Salt and freshly ground pepper

Chopped fresh cilantro for serving

In a soup pot, heat the olive oil over medium heat. Add the onion and sauté until beginning to soften and look translucent, 3 to 4 minutes. Add the garlic and cook for 1 minute longer.

Add the sweet potato and chipotle pepper to the pot. Add the stock and return to a boil, then reduce the heat to medium-low and simmer until the potatoes are tender enough to cut easily with the side of a fork, about 20 minutes.

Remove the soup from the heat. Using an immersion blender directly in the pot, or in a blender, process the soup to a smooth purée. (If using a blender, work carefully in batches to make sure you do not to burn yourself with the hot liquid.)

Return the soup to the pot, if you used a blender. Taste and adjust the seasoning with salt and pepper (or adobo sauce for more spice, if you like). Ladle into bowls, sprinkle with the cilantro, and serve hot.

Note: Canned chipotle peppers in adobo sauce are a wonderful, inexpensive pantry item found in any Latin foods store or supermarket. Chipotles are dried, smoked jalapeño chiles and adobo sauce is a sweet and tangy tomato-based sauce laced with garlic and spices. The chiles are rehydrated in the sauce, and the resulting combo provides a full spectrum of condimental charms. If you've never cooked with chipotle peppers before, I recommend starting with ½ pepper, or the smallest pepper in the can that you can find; you can also moderate the heat by scraping the seeds out of the chile and discarding them. You can always add more kick later with cayenne or additional adobo sauce, but if you make the soup too spicy at any stage, there's no turning back.

spicy pumpkin chili

SERVES TWO OR THREE

When the weather starts to get cooler, there's nothing like a big, warm bowl of chili. I especially love this recipe, as it incorporates one of my favorite autumn flavors: pumpkin. I usually used canned pumpkin when I need pumpkin purée (rather than roasting a whole pumpkin and making my own) simply because it makes throwing this meal together easy and fast. This recipe won't use an entire can, so store the leftovers in an airtight container in the refrigerator for up to 1 week. I like to stir leftover pumpkin purée into hot cereal, soups, or risotto. You could also use it in place of sauce on a whole-wheat pizza, if you're feeling adventurous.

2 Tbsp olive oil

¼ cup [35 g] chopped yellow onion

½ red bell pepper, seeded and diced

3 cloves garlic, minced

1 chipotle pepper in adobo sauce

1 can [15 oz/430 g] diced tomatoes, with juices

½ cup [120 g] pumpkin purée

¼ tsp ground cumin

1 can [15 oz/430 g] pinto beans, rinsed and drained well

1 can [15 oz/430 g] red beans, rinsed and drained well

Salt and freshly ground pepper

Vegetable stock, tomato sauce, or water, as needed

Baked corn tortilla chips, homemade (page 106) or store-bought, for serving

2 Tbsp chopped green onion

In a soup pot, heat the olive oil over medium heat. Add the onion and bell pepper and sauté for 2 to 3 minutes, until they begin to soften. Stir in the garlic and cook for 1 minute longer.

Chop the chipotle pepper and add it to the pot, and stir in a little of the sauce, too. Add the tomatoes and their juices, the pumpkin, and the cumin. Cook, stirring, for 2 to 3 minutes, to allow the flavors to blend.

Add the beans to the pot, stir well, and cook for another 3 to 4 minutes. When everything is hot, season with salt and pepper. I like my chili on the thick side, but if you prefer, you can thin it with splashes of vegetable stock, tomato sauce, or even water; start with about ¼ cup [60 ml].

To serve, ladle into bowls over the tortilla chips. Top with the green onions and serve hot.

tempeh taco salad with salsa and spicy mayo

SERVES TWO

This recipe is an adaptation of a salad served at one of my favorite bars in my hometown—a bar far better known for their whiskey cocktails and beer selection, but I swooned over this salad the first time I tasted it. And later I realized that with just a few minor tweaks, it could become a Weekday favorite. One of the things I love most about this salad: it's hearty! You won't walk away feeling hungry after eating this.

I make my own baked corn tortilla chips for this salad, or almost anytime. Many friends and family members tested all of the recipes in this book, and one tester was adamant: the homemade chips really make this salad. I could not agree with her more. But I realize that we are all often pressed for time, and you may want to throw this together quickly; you can certainly use store-bought corn tortilla chips instead. But if you have the time, make more than this recipe calls for, so you have extras to snack on throughout the week; the difference is so worth it!

FOR THE SPICY MAYO:

⅓ cup [80 g] mayonnaise, store-bought (no sugar added) or homemade (page 125)

1 to 2 Tbsp hot sauce (see Note, page 106)

8 oz [230 g] tempeh

1 to 2 Tbsp olive oil

⅓ cup [45 g] chopped red onion

Salt and freshly ground pepper

3 cloves garlic, minced

½ head lettuce (or more if you want even more veggies), chopped

¼ cup [60 g] salsa (no-sugar-added store-bought, or make your own)

1 to 2 Tbsp chopped fresh cilantro

½ cup [20 g] Baked Corn Tortillas (see Note, page 106), crushed

continued . . .

To make the Spicy Mayo, in a small bowl, stir together the mayo and hot sauce. Set aside.

Cube the tempeh. (It will crumble more as you cook it, so it's OK to cut into larger cubes.) Set aside.

In a saucepan, heat the olive oil over medium heat. Add the onion and sauté until translucent and lightly golden, about 5 minutes. Add the tempeh and season everything generously with salt and pepper. Cook for another 3 to 4 minutes, tossing gently but often so everything gets nice and hot. If things start to stick to the pan, add a little more oil. If the tempeh doesn't crumble as much as you'd like, use a wooden spoon or metal spatula (whatever you are working with) to break it up a little more in the pan. Add the garlic and sauté for 1 minute longer. Remove from the heat.

To assemble the salads, divide the lettuce between 2 salad plates or large shallow bowls. Arrange the warm tempeh mix on top, dividing it evenly, then garnish each serving with salsa, cilantro, crushed tortillas, and the Spicy Mayo. Serve immediately.

Note: My favorite hot sauce is Cholula, but any brand that doesn't contain hidden sugars is OK.

Note: For Baked Corn Tortillas, preheat the oven to 400°F [200°C]. Cut as many corn tortillas as you like into chip-size triangles. Pile on a baking sheet and toss with a little olive oil and salt. Spread in a single layer on the pan and bake until the edges begin to look crispy and turn a deep brown, 10 to 14 minutes, stirring once halfway through baking.

stacked apple and kale salad

SERVES TWO

This salad is not only delicious, it's also very pretty in its presentation. Usually I don't plate our dinners at home as if I'm working in a fancy restaurant—for example, I'm not overly careful with sauces or garnishes. To me, home cooking tends to be more about things like how long a dish takes to make, how many dishes it will dirty in the process, and how good it tastes. But every now and again, it's exciting to make something that is as pretty to serve as it is to eat—like this salad. If you can't be bothered to stack the ingredients into a towering, gorgeous heap, well I can't force you. Just chop everything up, if you must; you will still be able to enjoy the flavors all the same. But if you can be bothered, I think you'll remember that it's sometimes kind of fun to play with your food.

This salad is best consumed within an hour of making it, as the kale may soften too much and become unpleasantly wilted. If you need to make this dish a few hours ahead of time, hold off on dressing the kale or peeling the apple until just before you are ready to serve.

Serve with some whole-wheat toast or a small serving of soup.

¼ cup [35 g] shelled pistachio nuts

¼ cup [60 g] mayonnaise, store-bought (no sugar added) or homemade (page 125)

1 Tbsp raw honey

1 Tbsp fresh lemon juice

1 clove garlic, minced

Salt and freshly ground pepper

2½ cups [45 g] chopped kale (see Note, page 109)

1 Granny Smith apple

In a food processor, pulse the pistachios until well chopped. You can do this by hand if you prefer, but we're going for well chopped here, not a rough chop. You want the pieces quite small so you don't have a big crunch in the salad—but be careful not to overprocess them, or they'll get buttery. Set aside.

continued . . .

In a large bowl, stir together the mayo, honey, lemon juice, and garlic. Taste and adjust the seasoning with salt and pepper. Add the kale to the bowl and stir so all the kale pieces are well coated in the dressing.

Peel and core the apple, making sure the entire stem and all seeds have been removed. Then cut the apple into 8 slices. If you are not going to stack your salad then after peeling and removing the core you can simply cube the apple into bite-sized pieces.

To serve, place 1 slice of apple on each of 2 salad plates. Top each with a big spoonful of dressed kale, and then a sprinkle of pistachios. Repeat the entire process until 2 servings are completely plated. Serve immediately.

Note: Rinse and pat dry the kale. Remove the big center veins as well as any other veins that don't excite you to chew through. Really chop the kale into very small pieces and give it all a big squeeze with your clean hands. Some recipes will instruct you to massage kale to soften it a bit, and that's exactly what we are going for by giving it a good squeeze.

lots-of-broccoli pasta salad

SERVES TWO TO THREE AS A MAIN COURSE, OR FOUR TO FIVE AS A SIDE

This broccoli and whole-wheat pasta salad is a total staple at our house. It's creamy, sweet, salty, and full of delicious and crunchy broccoli. I'll make a big bowl of this for dinner for my husband and me, and then usually end up with a little extra for a work lunch the next day. This would also be a great dish to take to a backyard potluck (if you are lucky enough to live in a part of the world where that is a thing—if not, consider starting the tradition and see if it catches among your group of friends!).

This is a dish you can make hours before; it needs to be well chilled. Just refrigerate the components until you're ready to serve, then toss together. It's best consumed within 24 hours of making.

6 oz [170 g] whole-wheat pasta such as fusilli, farfalle, or penne

2 to 3 broccoli crowns, cut into bite-sized florets

5 pitted dates, chopped

½ cup [60 g] sliced almonds or other chopped nuts

⅓ cup [80 g] mayonnaise, store-bought (no sugar added) or homemade (page 125)

1 Tbsp date syrup or honey (see recipe introduction on page 126)

1 clove garlic, minced

1 tsp capers, plus 1 Tbsp brine from the capers jar

Salt and freshly ground pepper

Bring a pot of salted water to a boil. Add the pasta and cook until al dente according to the package directions. Drain well, reserving some of the cooking water. Set aside and let cool to room temperature.

In a large bowl, combine the pasta, broccoli, chopped dates, and almonds and toss to mix well. Set aside.

To make a dressing, in a small bowl, whisk together the mayo, date syrup, garlic, capers and caper brine, and 1 Tbsp of the reserved pasta-cooking water. If the dressing seems too thick, add another 1 Tbsp or so pasta water. (BTW, if you forgot to reserve the pasta water, don't worry—you can just use fresh water. The pasta water will be slightly thicker and starchier, which is why it works great here, but don't sweat it if you forgot.)

Pour the dressing over the broccoli mixture. Toss gently until everything is well coated. Taste and adjust the seasoning with salt and pepper. Cover and refrigerate until well-chilled, about 2 hours. Serve cold.

stuffed peppers with quinoa and black beans

SERVES TWO

More often than I care to admit, I cruise down the produce section at my grocery store grabbing all the same things I always get. I think many of us have this problem—and that's part of the reason why the number-one rule in Weekday Weekend is to eat a variety of things! Getting into a grocery-store rut is a great way to get bored with your meals fast. And that's one of the reasons that I love this recipe, as it forces me to reach past those red bell peppers I always grab and instead pick up a few poblanos instead. In this recipe, the pepper skins get smoky and slightly sweet while the flesh transforms into yummy succulence. Think of these as close kin to the usual veggies burrito; except that in place of a big, flour tortilla, you have a tender-crisp pepper shell instead.

If you make this recipe on the weekend, feel free to top the peppers with a little sour cream, too.

2 large poblano peppers

1 can [15 oz/430 g] black beans, rinsed and drained well

1½ cups [275 g] cooked quinoa

¼ tsp ground cumin

Salt and freshly ground pepper

2 Tbsp sunflower seeds

2 Tbsp hemp hearts (see Note, page 114)

2 cloves garlic

½ tsp salt

½ tsp chili powder

Big pinch of cayenne pepper

1 ripe avocado, pitted, peeled, and sliced

1 Tbsp chopped fresh cilantro

Salsa or hot sauce (no sugar added) for serving

continued . . .

Preheat the broiler.

Cut each pepper in half lengthwise. Remove the steam, membranes, and seeds. Place on a baking sheet, cut-side down, and broil until the skins begin to blacken, about 2 minutes.

Meanwhile, in a bowl, combine the black beans, quinoa, cumin, and salt and pepper to taste and toss to mix well.

In a food processor, combine the sunflower seeds, hemp hearts, garlic, salt, chili powder, and cayenne. Pulse until very crumbly but not completely ground (or buttery).

Remove the peppers from the oven and turn the oven temperature to 375°F [190°C]. Using tongs, turn the peppers skin-side down on the pan and fill each with the black bean and quinoa mixture, then top with the spicy nut topping.

Bake until hot throughout, 18 to 20 minutes. Remove from the oven and top with the avocado slices and cilantro. Serve warm with your favorite salsa or hot sauce, or both.

Note: Hemp hearts, also known as shelled hemp seeds from the hemp plant (a completely innocent cousin of the more notorious cannabis plant), are an excellent source of omega-3, fiber, and other nutrients. Even more, hemp hearts are one of the best non-animal complete sources of protein, packing in more protein per serving than flax or chia seeds. Their mild, nutty flavor makes them easy to incorporate into recipes: add a spoonful of hemp hearts to smoothies, homemade granola bars, or substitute for any dry ingredient for an added boost of nutrition! This ingredient has become quite popular and can be found at most grocery stores and health food markets.

steel-cut oats and sunflower-seed risotto [aka ris-oat-toe]

SERVES TWO AS A MAIN COURSE, OR FOUR AS A SIDE

For years and years now, I have been making risotto at home. One of the first times I served this dish to my husband, he didn't even realize it was any different from the usual cheesy Arborio rice risotto I often make—which I took to be a great review! With this Weekday recipe, you still get the creamy texture that you expect from risotto, but with the added benefits of whole-grain oats and nuts. You do need to soak the sunflower seeds first, so that they will take on that creamy, risotto-like texture. If you plan to make this for dinner, simply pour the seeds into a small bowl with water during your breakfast routine. This will give the seeds enough time to soak all day and be ready for a creamy dinner that night.

This is a great dish to serve alongside a vegetable side dish such as pan-fried asparagus or My Favorite Baked Brussels Sprouts (page 132).

2 Tbsp olive oil

3 Tbsp finely chopped yellow onion

3 cloves garlic, minced

½ cup [80 g] steel-cut oats

3 to 3½ cups [720 to 840 ml] vegetable stock, homemade or good-quality low-sodium store-bought

1 cup [140 g] frozen peas, thawed

⅔ cup [90 g] sunflower seeds, soaked in water to cover for 6 to 8 hours, then drained

1½ Tbsp Non-Dairy Basil Pesto (page 127)

2 Tbsp Non-Dairy Parmesan (page 128), plus more for serving

Salt and freshly ground pepper

Extra-virgin olive oil for drizzling

continued . . .

In a large saucepan, heat the olive oil over medium-high heat. Add the onion and cook, stirring, until softened, 2 to 3 minutes. Add the garlic and cook for 1 minute longer.

Add the oats and stir to coat with the oil. Add ½ cup [4 fl oz/120 ml] stock and cook, stirring, until the liquid begins to be absorbed into the oats mixture. When most of the liquid has been absorbed, add more stock in increments of about ½ cup [120 ml], waiting until each addition is absorbed before you add more. When you've added a total of about 3 cups [720 ml] of stock, taste the oats to check for doneness. If the oats aren't almost perfectly tender, add a bit more stock and continue cooking

When the oats are nearly cooked through, add the peas, sunflower seeds, pesto, and Parmesan. Cook until everything is warmed through. If your risotto begins to dry out, add a splash more stock or water. Season with salt and pepper.

To serve, divide among individual plates and drizzle with extra-virgin olive oil. Sprinkle with Parmesan and serve immediately.

stir-fried cabbage with wild rice and smoky coconut

SERVES TWO

My mom turned me on to stir-frying cabbage. She made a version of this dish when I was growing up, and when I graduated from my I-only-eat-peanut-butter-sandwiches-and-macaroni-and-cheese phase, I found that I really loved the soft-but-still-crunchy texture. It's totally delicious, easy to throw together, and packs a big serving of vegetables.

2 Tbsp olive oil

3 Tbsp chopped yellow onion

½ head cabbage, about 1 lb [455 g], cored and shredded

3 cloves garlic, minced

1 Tbsp soy sauce

1 Tbsp miso (see Note, page 25)

1 cup [180 g] cooked wild rice, or a mixture of brown and wild rice

Salt and freshly ground pepper

2 to 3 Tbsp Smoky Coconut Flakes (page 129), optional

In a large skillet or wok, heat the olive oil over medium-high heat. Add the onion and cook until softened, about 2 minutes. Add the cabbage and cook, stirring, until coated with the oil and wilted, 3 to 4 minutes. Add the garlic and cook for 1 minute longer.

In a small bowl, stir together the soy sauce and miso. Set aside. When the cabbage is softened but still holding most of its color, push all of the vegetables to one side of the pan. Spoon the cooked rice into the empty side of the pan. Pour the soy sauce mixture over the rice and stir everything together until warmed through. Taste and adjust the seasoning with salt and pepper.

To serve, divide the stir-fry between individual plates or bowls. Top with the coconut, if using, and serve immediately.

snow pea and pineapple stir-fry with cauliflower rice

SERVES TWO

This is a great meal to try if you feel like you just haven't eaten enough veggies that day. Don't fret—it happens. An easy remedy: Just throw this quick and delicious meal together for you and a loved one. This recipe uses cauliflower rice instead of any true grains, a fun alternative that makes it extra light. But to be honest, my very favorite thing about this meal is that once your veggies are prepped, you only have to wait about 10 minutes for dinner to be ready.

1 head cauliflower, about 1½ lb [680 g], cored and cut into chunks

2 tsp olive oil, plus more if needed

2 Tbsp chopped onion

1 red or orange bell pepper, seeded and cut into matchsticks

4 oz [115 g] snow peas

1 cup [140 g] fresh cubed pineapple

2 cloves garlic, minced

3 Tbsp soy sauce

1 Tbsp honey or pure maple syrup

2 tsp sesame oil

¼ tsp red pepper flakes

2 Tbsp chopped raw cashew nuts

1 Tbsp chopped green onion

Put the cauliflower in a food processor and pulse until processed into very small uniform pieces resembling rice. (You may need to do this in a few batches, depending on the size of your processor. Be careful not to pulse so much that you turn your cauliflower into a purée.) Transfer to a plate lined with a couple of layers of paper towels to absorb excess moisture. Set aside.

In a large skillet or wok, warm the olive oil over medium heat. Add the onion and bell pepper and cook, stirring, until softened, for about 2 minutes. Add the snow peas, pineapple, and garlic and cook, stirring often, for another 2 minutes. Add a little more oil to the pan if needed to prevent sticking.

Meanwhile, in a small bowl, stir together the soy sauce, honey, sesame oil, and red pepper flakes.

Add the cauliflower rice to the pan with the other vegetables and stir to combine, then pour the sauce over everything. Give it a stir and cook for another 2 minutes to heat everything through. Add the cashews and green onion and toss and stir for 1 minute longer.

To serve, divide the stir-fry between individual plates and serve hot.

black rice sushi bowls

SERVES TWO

This meal reminds me a lot of avocado rolls, which I love. But if you want to add more steamed or lightly sautéed veggies or a fried egg on top, go for it!

¾ cup [150 g] black rice

8 oz [230 g] extra-firm tofu

1 Tbsp arrowroot powder (see Note, page 35)

1 Tbsp sesame oil

2 Tbsp soy sauce

⅛ tsp garlic powder

⅛ tsp ground ginger

¼ tsp red pepper flakes

1 ripe avocado, pitted, peeled, and sliced

1 sheet nori, sliced (use kitchen shears or scissors to get super-thin pieces)

1 Tbsp sesame seeds, toasted (see Note, page 133)

Preheat the oven to 350°F [180°C].

Meanwhile, steam the black rice according to the package directions.

Drain the tofu from the liquid in its package. Place on a plate lined with a double thickness of paper towel. Place another paper towel on top of the tofu, then a second plate on top of that. Finally, place something heavy on top, like a large can of tomatoes (or whatever you have on hand). Let the tofu drain under pressure for 10 minutes. Remove the tofu from the paper towels and weights and cut into small cubes. Transfer to a large zippered plastic bag or a bowl, sprinkle with the arrowroot, and toss to coat well. (I prefer the zippered bag technique.) Spread the dusted tofu on a baking sheet, transfer to the oven, and bake until slightly hardened and the edges begin to look crispy, 25 to 35 minutes.

Just before the tofu and rice are both ready, in a microwave-safe bowl, stir together the sesame oil, soy sauce, garlic powder, ginger, and red pepper flakes. Microwave on high for 30 seconds, or just until hot. (You could also do this in a small saucepan on the stovetop.)

To assemble the sushi bowls, divide the steamed black rice between 2 large individual serving bowls. Arrange the sliced avocado, baked tofu, nori, and sesame seeds on top, dividing them evenly. Pour the sauce over everything and serve immediately.

A Beautiful Mess

homemade mayonnaise

MAKES ABOUT TWO CUPS [480 G]

In my mind there are two reasons why you might want to make your own mayonnaise, and that's why I've included a recipe here for you to try. First, it may be difficult for you to find a store-bought version that does not contain added sugars or other ingredients you are looking to avoid. But second, making your own allows you to customize and change the mayonnaise in ways that you may prefer. What oil (or oils) you use here can really change the flavor. I like to use a mix of 1 cup [240 ml] peanut oil and ⅓ cup [80 ml] olive oil most of the time. But feel free to experiment with different oils to see what you like best. The only oil I would avoid is coconut oil; because it is solid oil at room temperature, it can really throw off the texture of the mayo. You have to be patient; the key is to add the oil slowly so it can emulsify to the perfect silky consistency.

3 large egg yolks, separated
  (see Note)
½ tsp salt
1⅓ cups [320 ml] oil (see
  recipe introduction)
1 Tbsp white vinegar or
  fresh lemon juice
Freshly ground pepper

In the bowl of a stand mixer, combine 2 of the egg yolks and the salt and whisk until well blended and thick. With the mixer running on low, begin to drip the oil very slowly into the egg yolks until you've incorporated about two-thirds of the oil into the yolks, 12 to 15 minutes.

In a separate bowl, whisk the remaining egg yolk until well blended. Start the mixer again and slowly add the egg yolk to the mix. Now add the remaining one-third of the oil in a slow steady stream. When all the oil is incorporated,

stir in the vinegar. Taste and adjust the seasoning with salt and pepper.

Store in an airtight container in the refrigerator for up to 2 weeks.

Note: First, separate the eggs. Eggs are easiest to separate when they are cold, but you actually want your eggs at room temperature for this recipe. What to do? Rinse two bowls (or one bowl and one ramekin) in hot water. Dry with a paper towel. Separate the eggs while still cold from the fridge, placing two yolks in one warm bowl and one yolk in another. It's OK if your yolks break.

If you like, pour the oil into a squirt bottle. Using a squirt bottle really helps make sure you don't add too much oil at once.

homemade bbq sauce

MAKES ABOUT TWO-AND-A-HALF CUPS [600 ML]

Elsie and I both grew up in southern Missouri, where barbecue is a BIG deal. Folks can become very loyal to certain brands, and have also been known to trash-talk the competition—all in good fun, of course. I loved the idea of including some recipes that use this delicious condiment, but the majority of the time they are made with a hefty amount of added sugar. Here I worked to develop a BBQ sauce that doesn't include as much, and what's here is kept so that we aren't missing out on any of the delicious flavors that define the sauce.

Date syrup is made simply from pressed dates and is a fantastic healthier alterative to processed syrup and liquid sweeteners. Similar to molasses in its deep, rich sweetness, date syrup can easily be used in both sweet (think drizzled on ice cream or yogurt) and savory (added to your favorite glaze recipe) meals. It can be found at most specialty grocery stores and in your local Middle Eastern market.

1 Tbsp olive oil

1 yellow onion, chopped

4 cloves garlic, minced

2 cups [520 g] ketchup
  (no sugar added)

⅓ cup [105 g] molasses

3 Tbsp pure maple syrup

3 Tbsp date syrup
  (see recipe introduction)

¼ cup [60 ml] apple cider vinegar

1 Tbsp dry mustard

1 Tbsp chili powder

½ tsp cayenne pepper

⅛ tsp ground cinnamon

Salt and freshly ground
  black pepper

In a saucepan or skillet, heat the olive oil. Add the onion and sauté until very soft and lightly golden, 5 to 6 minutes. Add the garlic and cook for 2 minutes longer.

Transfer the onion mixture to a food processor or blender and add the ketchup, molasses, maple syrup, date syrup, vinegar, mustard, chili powder, cayenne, and cinnamon. Process until smooth.

Transfer the sauce to a heavy-bottomed saucepan and cook over medium heat for about 30 minutes. If the sauce starts sticking to the sides of the pan, lower the heat a little. Towards the end of cooking, the sauce should thicken and become very fragrant. Taste and adjust the seasoning with salt and black pepper. Remove from the heat and let cool.

Store in an airtight container in the refrigerator for up to 3 weeks.

non-dairy basil pesto

MAKES ABOUT ONE CUP [240 G]

Pesto is such an amazing ingredient. You can use it as a pizza sauce, toss with pasta and a few vegetables for a quick meal, or spread over bread to enhance a sandwich. As it's comprised mainly of basil, it certainly packs a flavorful punch. The only issue is most commercial options include dairy (cheese). You may be able to find a version that can work for weekday recipes but if you have trouble just make your own—it's super easy and will taste SO fresh.

1½ cups [30 g] packed basil leaves
¼ cup [30 g] pine nuts
2 Tbsp nutritional yeast (see Note)
1 clove garlic, coarsely chopped
1 tsp salt
½ to ⅔ cup [120 to 160 ml] olive oil

In a blender or food processor, combine the basil, pine nuts, nutritional yeast, garlic, and salt and pulse to mix. With the machine running, drizzle in the oil in a slow steady stream until a coarse, uniform purée forms. Stop the machine to scrape down the sides of the jar or work bowl as needed.

Store in an airtight container in the refrigerator for up to 2 weeks. You can also fill an ice cube tray with the pesto and freeze into cubes for use later.

Note: Nutritional yeast is made by pasteurizing and drying the same strain of yeast used in baking bread. It's the perfect substitute for cheese, with a deeply savory, umami flavor. Formed into flakes or powder for easy use, you can usually find nutritional yeast in the bulk section at any natural food store and most major grocery chains. Nutritional yeast is known for its B vitamin content, although this varies depending on how it's made as sometimes the vitamins are added by fortification (adding nutrients not normally present in the food). Either way, it is a good alternative to many seasonings that contain questionable preservatives and anti-caking agents. Use it to add cheesy, nutty goodness with little guilt: mixed into scrambles, sprinkled on top of your favorite savory snack (avocado toast, anyone?), or blended into pesto.

non-dairy parmesan

MAKES ABOUT ONE CUP [90 G]

I know what you're thinking, "Non-Dairy Parmesan? What in the world does that even mean?" Yes, it's a bit of an oxymoron I will admit. But, the flavor is somewhat similar to cheese due to the nutritional yeast and you will soon find yourself adding this in much the same way you would Parmesan. It's delicious on top of pizza, soups, salads, popcorn, or pasta dishes.

½ cup [70 g] raw cashew nuts

2 Tbsp hemp hearts
   (see Note, page 114)

¼ cup [18 g] nutritional yeast
   (see Note, page 127)

1 tsp salt

¼ tsp garlic powder

⅛ tsp onion powder

Combine all of the ingredients in a blender or food processor and process until a uniform powdery grind forms. Store in an airtight container for up to 2 weeks.

smoky coconut flakes

MAKES ABOUT ONE CUP [60 G]

Coconut is such an amazing ingredient. The cream and milk can be used in soups, curries, or whipped into a topping for sweet dishes. Here we flavor and bake coconut flakes to use in much the same way you might use bacon bites. If you love these as much as we do, double the recipe and use in all sorts of weekday (or weekend) recipes: to add texture and flavor to stir fries, soups, salads, sandwiches—the list goes on and on!

3 tsp soy sauce

2 tsp liquid smoke

2 tsp molasses

2 tsp sesame seed oil

2 tsp apple cider vinegar

½ tsp salt

¼ tsp ground cumin

1 cup [80 g] unsweetened coconut flakes

Preheat the oven to 325°F [165°C].

In a bowl, whisk together the soy sauce, liquid smoke, molasses, sesame seed oil, apple cider vinegar, salt, and cumin.

Add the coconut flakes and stir until well coated. Let sit for 5 minutes so that the coconut begins to absorb the liquids. Spread on a baking sheet in a single layer and bake, tossing every 3 to 5 minutes, until dark brown and very crispy looking, 10 to 12 minutes total. Remove from the oven to a wire rack and let cool completely.

Store in an airtight container for up to 2 weeks. If the coconut flakes begin to feel soft or soggy, you can re-toast them in the oven for a few minutes at 325°F [165°C].

creamy mashed cauliflower

SERVES TWO OR THREE AS A SIDE

Like mashed potatoes, only better.

1 head cauliflower, cored and
  cut into wedges
3 tsp olive oil
Salt and freshly ground pepper
1 head garlic
1 to 2 tablespoons almond milk,
  if needed

Preheat the oven to 400°F [200°C].

Pile the cauliflower on a large baking sheet lined with parchment paper or a silicone baking mat. Drizzle with 2 tsp of the olive oil, season with salt and paper, and toss to coat well. Spread the cauliflower in a single layer on the pan.

Slice off the top [about ¼ in/6 mm] of the garlic head. Drizzle the remaining 1 tsp olive oil on the exposed garlic cloves. Wrap the entire head in foil and tuck into a corner of the same baking sheet with the cauliflower.

Bake for 20 to 25 minutes, until the cauliflower is quite soft. Transfer the cauliflower pieces and the garlic cloves (remove the foil and any of the papery layers from the head) to a food processor or blender and process until smooth. If the texture seems grainy, add a tablespoon or two of almond milk and process again until you have a creamy, mashed cauliflower purée. Serve warm.

A Beautiful Mess

my favorite baked brussels sprouts

SERVES TWO AS A SIDE

The lemon juice really makes these pop with flavor.

15 Brussels sprouts [435 g], trimmed and halved

1½ Tbsp olive oil

½ tsp salt

1 lemon

Preheat the oven to 400°F [200°C].

In a large bowl, toss the Brussels sprouts with the olive oil so that all the sprouts get well coated with the oil. Transfer to a baking sheet and arrange cut-side down. Sprinkle the salt over the sprouts.

Bake until tender with some crispy edges, 16 to 20 minutes. (I usually bake mine for almost 20 minutes, but I must confess, I like my Brussels sprouts quite crispy—some might say a little burnt. So if this is your first time preparing them this way, check them at 16 minutes and see what you think.)

Remove the sprouts from the oven and immediately squeeze fresh lemon juice all over them. Serve hot.

garlic-miso asparagus

SERVES TWO TO THREE AS A SIDE

A little miso adds a "what is it?" umami quality here, bringing together the salt in the soy, the warmth of the garlic, and that unique asparagus tang.

1 bunch asparagus, about 1 lb [455 g]
2 Tbsp olive oil
1 Tbsp soy sauce
1 Tbsp miso (see Note, page 25)
2 tsp sesame oil
4 cloves garlic, minced
1 Tbsp toasted sesame seeds or chopped nuts (optional, see Note)

Snap the tough woody end off each asparagus stalk, bending the stalks until they snap naturally at the point where the tender spear begins.

In a large skillet or wok, heat the olive oil over medium-high heat. Add the asparagus and cook, tossing and stirring, until bright green and just beginning to soften, 2 to 3 minutes.

Meanwhile, in a small bowl, stir together the soy sauce, miso, and sesame oil. Set aside.

Add the garlic to the pan with the asparagus and cook, stirring, for 1 minute longer. Pour the soy sauce mixture over the asparagus and stir for another minute.

Divide the asparagus between 2 plates, drizzle the sauce over, and garnish with the sesame seeds, if using. Serve warm.

Note: Cultivated from the plant of the same name, little sesame seeds pack in big health benefits. They're rich in minerals like calcium and potassium, high in dietary fiber, and are a source of healthy polyunsaturated fats. Most often used as a main ingredient for tahini or sprinkled on foods for a light, nutty crunch, sesame seeds are easily found in any major grocery store's spice or bulk section or at your local Middle Eastern market. To toast sesame seeds, add to a skillet over medium heat and cook, stirring often, until golden brown, 3 to 4 minutes.

A Beautiful Mess

garlicky sweet potato bites

SERVES TWO OR THREE AS A SIDE

You can prepare this up to three days ahead and store in the refrigerator if you like, to cut back on prep time. Just form the little patties and cook when you are ready. This is one of my favorite sides as it's very substantial and really tasty from the garlic and sweet potato flavors blending together.

1 large sweet potato, about 1 lb [455 g], cooked and mashed (see Note)

1 cup [120 g] almond meal

1 large egg yolk

3 cloves garlic, minced

2 tsp olive oil, plus 1 Tbsp olive oil

Salt and freshly ground pepper

1 Tbsp chopped green onion

In a bowl, mash together the sweet potato, almond meal, egg yolk, garlic, and the 2 tsp olive oil. Form 12 to 15 small balls or patties from the batter. (If the batter won't hold together, place the entire bowl, covered in plastic wrap, in the refrigerator for 15 minutes to allow it to firm up.)

In a large skillet, heat the 1 Tbsp olive oil over medium-high heat. Working in batches to avoid crowding, pan-fry the sweet potato bites, turning once, until crisp on the edges and very fragrant, 2 to 3 minutes per side. Transfer each batch to a serving plate as they are finished.

When all the bites are cooked, season with salt and pepper, garnish with green onions, and serve immediately.

Note: To bake sweet potatoes, preheat the oven to 375°C [190°C]. Scrub the potatoes and dry thoroughly. Poke a few holes in the top of each with a fork, to allow steam to escape, and place on a baking sheet. Bake until very tender when pierced with the fork or a thin-bladed knife, about 45 minutes, depending on the size and age of the potatoes. Let cool slightly, then remove the potato from the skins. Chop, slice, or mash as needed. Leftover baked sweet potato will keep, covered tightly in the fridge, for up to 3 days, or freeze in freezer bags or ice cube trays to preserve them for longer periods.

A Beautiful Mess

WEEKEND

I'll be honest: After a couple months of eating the Weekday Weekend way, my cravings and taste buds changed. At first I thought I'd spend every weekend eating nothing but white bread with sugar sprinkled over the top, like an addict. But, thankfully, my body surprised me. What I mean is, although we can technically eat anything we want over the weekend, I don't usually feel like filling every single meal with copious amounts of sugar, dairy, and alcohol. That's not to say I don't get my treats in! But a lot of my weekend meals consist of my husband and I going out, or I'll often make a Weekday meal but just slightly change it for Weekend fun. For example, our whole-wheat pizza crust recipe is one of my very favorite pizza crusts during the week, but I use the same recipe on the weekend; I just add cheese to my pizza for a change and an extra-special treat. Feel free to change up any of your favorite Weekday meals along those lines. But here we have included a few extra-decadent recipes for you to try, as well.

crispy baked fries in mushroom gravy

SERVES TWO AS A MAIN COURSE, OR FOUR AS A STARTER

This is total comfort food, as it combines three delicious elements: potatoes, gravy, and cheese. Whoa. This recipe is sort of a homemade vegetarian version of poutine. You can make this dish using both russet and sweet potatoes as recommended in the recipe below, or you can use all russet. You could even simply buy a bag of frozen premade French fries and focus your cooking efforts only on the gravy, if you want to make this even easier. You got options! But no matter which way you go, you will end up with a truly Weekend-worthy meal.

These loaded fries are best consumed right away, since once gravy gets cold, it's just not as good. I sometimes like to serve them in two small cast iron dishes or larger bowls so the gravy gets a little more contained than on a plate—but you can do what you like here.

1 large russet potato, about 12 oz [340 g]

1 large sweet potato, about 12 oz [340 g]

3 Tbsp olive oil

Salt and freshly ground black pepper

FOR THE GRAVY:

4 Tbsp [55 g] unsalted butter

2 Tbsp all-purpose flour

½ oz [15 g] dried wild mushrooms (I love porcini for this recipe), soaked, rinsed, and drained well, then chopped

1 cup [240 ml] vegetable stock, homemade or good-quality low-sodium store-bought

Big pinch of cayenne pepper

Big pinch of ground cumin

Salt and freshly ground black pepper

1 cup [80 g] cheese curds or shredded white Cheddar cheese

2 Tbsp chopped fresh herbs such as parsley, chives, or cilantro, or a combination

continued . . .

Preheat the oven to 450°F [230°C].

Peel the potatoes and cut into fries. Try to keep all the pieces as uniform as you can so they will bake evenly. Soak in a large bowl of water for 20 minutes.

(While the potatoes are soaking, check the package instructions on your dried wild mushrooms. Likely it will instruct you to soak the mushrooms in water for 20 to 30 minutes before rinsing well and then they are ready to use. Now is a great time to begin this process.)

Drain the potatoes and pat dry with paper towels. Line a large baking sheet with paper towels and spread out the fries on the lined pan in one layer, then pat the tops with another layer of paper towels. You want the fries to be really dry. Place in a clean, dry large bowl and toss with 1 Tbsp of the olive oil. Pour the other 2 Tbsp of olive oil over a dry large baking sheet and spread so the entire pan is coated in oil. Add the fries to the baking sheet, spread in a single layer, and season generously with salt and black pepper.

Cover the pan with aluminum foil and bake for 5 minutes. Carefully remove the foil and continue baking for another 12 minutes, until the edges of the fries begin to brown. Remove the pan from the oven and, using tongs, carefully turn each fry to make sure they aren't sticking to the pan, and also to help all sides get crispy. Once flipped, bake until the edges of the fries begin to turn a deep brown, 12 to 14 minutes longer.

During the last 10 minutes or so of baking time, make your gravy. First, make sure you have drained and rinsed your wild mushrooms. Then chop or cut with kitchen shears into small pieces and set aside.

In a saucepan, melt the butter over medium heat. Add the flour and whisk to make a roux (or, as I like to call it, "butter paste"). Turn the heat down to low and begin to slowly incorporate the mushrooms and vegetable stock, whisking constantly. Season with cayenne, cumin, plenty of salt, and black pepper. The mixture will thicken into a creamy gravy. If the gravy begins to seem too thick, turn the heat down (or off) and whisk to avoid lumps. If needed, add a little more vegetable stock, water, or even a little cream to thin it back to the consistency you want. If the gravy appears too thin, turn the heat up a little and continue to whisk, keeping a close eye on it so once it reaches the consistency you want you can turn the heat down or off so it doesn't thicken beyond that point.

When the fries are done, divide into servings and top with the cheese, then the gravy, and then the fresh herbs. Serve hot.

cheesy white wine risotto

SERVES TWO OR THREE

What do I love most about Weekend risotto? You might guess cheese, but you'd be wrong—it's the wine! And here's why: I don't use the entire bottle of wine in the risotto recipe. But with an already open bottle and a delicious dinner for two already prepared, I think the only logical conclusion is to split the remaining wine with your dinner partner. Maybe cuddle up on the couch with a comedy, too—oh yes, that's my kind of weekend.

20 to 25 asparagus spears
2 Tbsp olive oil
Salt and freshly ground pepper

1 cup [240 ml] dry white wine
  (see Note, page 141)
2⅔ cups [640 g] vegetable stock,
  homemade or good-quality
  low-sodium store-bought
2 Tbsp unsalted butter
⅓ cup [45 g] chopped white onion
3 cloves garlic, minced
1 cup [200 g] Arborio rice
½ cup [15 g] freshly grated
  Parmesan cheese

1 tsp chopped fresh thyme
1 tsp chopped fresh rosemary

Preheat the oven to 375°F [190°C].

Snap the tough woody end off each asparagus stalk, bending the stalks until they snap naturally at the point where the tender spear begins. Arrange the asparagus on a baking sheet. Toss the olive oil and season with salt and pepper. Roast until bright green and tender, 8 to 12 minutes. (Depending how soft you prefer your asparagus, you can adjust the bake time.)

Meanwhile, in a saucepan, combine the wine and vegetable stock. Simmer over very low heat. (Having these elements warm will help them cook into the risotto faster. This step is not absolutely necessary, but I find that this traditional technique does save me some time.)

continued . . .

In a large saucepan, melt the butter over medium-high heat. Add the onion and garlic and sauté just until they begin to soften and become very fragrant, 1 to 2 minutes. Add the rice and stir to coat all the grains in the fat. Cook until they begin to look translucent, about 2 minutes longer.

Now begin adding the stock mixture, ½ cup [120 ml] at a time, stirring until it's mostly absorbed before adding more. Continue until the rice is tender and cooked through. (I usually taste a few grains of rice once I've used most of the liquid. See if they feel uncooked to the bite in the center; if so continue cooking. You may not need all of the liquid, but you'll at least get close.)

When the rice is done, stir in the cheese. Taste and adjust the seasoning with salt and pepper.

To serve, arrange the roasted asparagus on individual plates and spoon the risotto alongside. Sprinkle the thyme and rosemary over everything and serve immediately.

Note: If you are opening a new bottle, choose something that you'd like to drink with dinner. Avoid sweet wines like Moscato or Riesling when cooking. I most often use a buttery Chardonnay, and almost always have one in my refrigerator in case we have unexpected guests—or I want to make risotto.

cream sauce pizza with raspberries and arugula

SERVES TWO TO FOUR

Even though we get to enjoy pizza during the week, there is one sauce that I really crave now and again that just doesn't work—creamy white sauce. There are probably about a million variations of this Alfredo-like sauce, but this is my favorite version. It's simple but very creamy and heavy on the garlic, which you may have realized by now is one of my favorite ingredients for both Weekday and Weekend cooking. (We should have named the book Start with Garlic.)

This sauce is lovely with a number of different toppings, but I highly recommend you try out the combination in this recipe first: raspberries and arugula. While it may sound odd, the raspberries add a bright, tart pop of flavor (and color), while the arugula adds an almost peppery kick. Plus, the fruit and green make us feel that we are at least eating something fresh and fiber-filled with this rich meal.

If you serve this pizza on its own, expect it to serve 2 to 3 adults, but if you want to stretch it further, serve it along with a salad or other vegetable side dish. You can use our weekday crust recipe on page 94; or, try swapping out some of the white whole-wheat flour in that recipe for all-purpose flour, for a slightly lighter and sweeter crust. Or use another recipe you love, or a good-quality purchased dough.

If you like, top the hot slices with a little more grated Parmesan, or a balsamic vinegar reduction.

continued . . .

A Beautiful Mess

1 recipe Whole-Wheat Pizza Crust (page 94), or your favorite recipe (see recipe introduction)

Olive oil for greasing

Whole-grain cornmeal for dusting (optional)

FOR THE SAUCE:

3 Tbsp unsalted butter

4 cloves garlic, minced

2 Tbsp all-purpose flour

¼ tsp onion powder

⅔ to 1 cup [160 to 240 ml] heavy cream or whole milk

1 Tbsp freshly grated Parmesan cheese

Salt and freshly ground pepper

FOR THE TOPPINGS:

1 cup [80 g] shredded fresh mozzarella cheese

⅔ cup [80 g] fresh raspberries

1 cup [20 g] packed arugula leaves

First, make your pizza dough. Towards the very end of the dough rise time, the last 15 minutes or so, preheat the oven to 400°F [200°C]. Oil a large baking sheet. Dust lightly with cornmeal, if using.

Meanwhile, make the sauce: In a saucepan over medium heat, melt the butter. Add the garlic and sauté until very fragrant, about 1 minute. Add the flour and onion powder and whisk until a roux forms. Reduce the heat to low and slowly whisk in the cream or whole milk, starting with ⅔ cup [160 ml]. Keep whisking over low heat until the sauce is thick enough to easily coat a spoon. If the sauce gets too thick, thin it with the remaining cream—just remove from the heat and whisk in the cream until you reach the desired consistency. Stir in the Parmesan. Taste and adjust the seasoning with salt and pepper.

When the dough is ready, roll it out on a lightly floured work surface. Transfer to the prepared baking sheet and bake for 5 minutes, then remove from the oven and top with the sauce, mozzarella, and raspberries. Return to the oven and bake until the mozzarella cheese is bubbly and beginning to brown, about 5 minutes. Top with arugula and put back in the oven for 1 minute longer, just to let the greens warm a little.

Cut into wedges and serve hot.

harissa margherita pizza

SERVES TWO TO FOUR

For a cookbook that's not supposed to be all about pizza, we clearly are OK adding a number of pizza recipes, aren't we? What can I say? I'm a pizza fanatic. And the weekend is a great time to enjoy pizza because: CHEESE! Glorious, glorious cheese. This pizza looks simple, but the harissa in the sauce adds complexity that you might not expect in a margherita pizza. It's a little spicy, a little sweet, and a whole lot delicious.

1 recipe Whole-Wheat Pizza Crust (page 94), or your favorite recipe (see recipe introduction on page 142)

Whole-grain cornmeal for dusting (optional)

FOR THE SAUCE:

1 tsp olive oil or unsalted butter

2 cloves garlic, minced

1 can [14½ oz/415 g] whole plum tomatoes, drained

2 Tbsp harissa (see Note, page 65)

Salt and freshly ground pepper

FOR THE TOPPINGS:

8 oz [230 g] fresh mozzarella cheese, shredded

2 oz [60 g] feta cheese, crumbled (optional, but really nice with this dish)

6 to 8 fresh basil leaves

First, make your pizza dough. Towards the very end of the dough rise time, the last 15 minutes or so, preheat the oven to 400°F [200°C]. Oil a large baking sheet. Dust lightly with cornmeal, if using.

Meanwhile, make the sauce: In a saucepan, heat the olive oil over medium heat. Add the garlic and sauté until very fragrant and just beginning to brown, 1 to 2 minutes. Transfer the garlic and oil to a blender or food processor and add the drained tomatoes and the harissa. Process to a smooth purée (or almost smooth—it's OK if there are still a few chunks, it just depends what texture you like your pizza sauce). Return to the saucepan and cook over medium heat until nicely thickened, 12 to 15 minutes. Taste and adjust the seasoning with salt and pepper. Remove from the heat and set aside.

continued . . .

When the dough is ready, roll it out on a lightly floured work surface. Transfer to the prepared baking sheet and bake for 5 minutes, then remove from the oven and top with the sauce, mozzarella, and feta, if using. Continue to bake until the mozzarella cheese is bubbly and beginning to brown, about 3 minutes. Top with thinly sliced or torn basil just before serving.

Cut into wedges and serve hot.

the ultimate cheese plate

SERVES AS MANY (OR AS FEW) AS YOU LIKE

There are very few things in life that make me as straight-up emotional as a good cheese plate. IT'S ART! So if you consider yourself a cheese enthusiast, take to heart the advice I'm about to give you: Why make an average cheese plate when you can make THE ULTIMATE cheese plate. Here's a checklist of everything I consider essential as well as extra credit!

Essentials:

- Sharp Cheddar cheese
- Goat cheese / chèvre
- Brie
- Boursin
- Water crackers
- Italian breadsticks
- Sliced baguette
- Nuts (I like a mix of savory and sweet. Rosemary roasted almonds and candied pecans are two of my favorites.)
- Olives (a mix of green and black, fleshy types and chewy and dry-cured)
- Honey (look for new and nuanced flavors like wildflower and acacia)

Bonus Points:

- A huge variety of crackers
- Blue cheese
- Crudités
- Mini mozzarella balls or Parmesan crisps
- Hummus
- Jams
- Sliced tart apples (Toss in a little fresh lemon juice if you are making this for a party and don't want them to brown too quickly.)
- Grapes (red or green and seedless are preferred but not mandatory)
- Fresh berries such as strawberries, blueberries, and/or raspberries

snac
swe

ks &
ets

WEEKDAY

Sometimes you just need a little something to get you through the hours until your next meal. Or you just want something snacky to enjoy while you unwind with your favorite TV program, but you don't want it to derail your healthy-eating mindset for the week. I think snacks and natural sweets that hit those cravings totally have a place in life! So here are a few of our favorite recipes.

from the nutritionists

Who doesn't love a good snack? I know we do. But, so many times last-minute snacking can steer us away from a healthy eating track. The key to healthy snacking is to have a plan in place before you get hungry. When we're talking about eating real food, this often means making your own snack items to keep on hand before cravings hit. The bottom line is: make sure you're prepared so you don't grab last-minute junk food. You'll always have a healthy snack: this is one of the many reasons we love this chapter. These recipes give you that little bite of sweet and are packed with fiber (which helps you feel full longer) and other key nutrients. And they're delicious! Mango-Coconut Ice Cream (page 159)? Come on!

Fiber

Adequate intake of fiber for 18 to 50 year olds is 26 grams for women and 38 grams for men each day according to the Institute of Medicine. However, when we're talking fiber, more is usually better. Fiber is so important, not only for fighting hunger and cravings, but also for preventing disease. The American Heart Association reports that eating high-fiber foods like whole grains may improve blood cholesterol levels, and lower risk of type 2 diabetes, stroke, heart disease, and obesity. Unfortunately, most of us are getting fewer than 10 grams. To get more we need to eat more 100 percent whole grains, fruit, vegetables, nuts, and seeds. A quick trick to ensure that you get enough fiber in your diet every day, is to break it down by meal. If you eat 3 meals per day, set a goal of getting 10 grams of fiber at each meal from the good sources cited above. In our experience, this makes it feel much more doable and is easier to keep track of.

Chia Seeds

What's the deal with those tiny things? Chia seeds are about the size of a sesame seed when dry, but add liquid and they expand to several times their original size. They form a really cool gel that not only serves as a natural thickener, but helps to make some of the good stuff in the seeds more usable by our bodies. These little superfoods' high fiber content is a fantastic benefit (see left) and they're a surprising source of protein at 2 grams per tablespoon. The most exciting thing about chia seeds is their omega-3 fat content. This is the anti-inflammatory fat that is out of balance with the much more common omega-6 fats found in high amounts in the modern, highly processed diet. The goal here is to get your ratio of omega-3 to omega-6 fats close to 1:1. For most, this means decreasing those oils high in omega-6 fats like soybean and corn oil found in many overly-processed foods and increasing your omega-3 fat intake from things like fatty fish, olive oil, and (you guessed it!) chia seeds. Cheers to that!

very berry chia pudding

SERVES TWO

Chia pudding has become pretty trendy in the last few years, but it's a little bit of an acquired texture. Not acquired taste, as while it does have a unique flavor, it's pretty mild … but the texture is something you may need to warm up to if you've never tried chia before. When chia seeds soak, they produce a kind of gel coating, so they work well if you want to make puddings, jams, or even just a thickener in a drink you enjoy. This pudding makes a great Weekday snack or even breakfast, and the addition of the raspberries or blackberries helps to add even more color and texture to chia pudding. So this is a great recipe to try if you've never had chia seeds before or you feel on the fence.

If you like, top the pudding with chopped nuts, toasted coconut flakes, more berries or other fruit, or even a scoop of banana ice cream if you really want to feel like you're having dessert!

1½ cups [180 g] fresh or frozen raspberries or blackberries, or a mixture of the two

1 cup [240 ml] unsweetened almond milk

1 Tbsp raw honey

¼ cup [45 g] chia seeds

In a blender, combine the berries, almond milk, and honey. Blend until smooth. If you are using frozen berries, thaw them first so you get a thinner consistency than you would if you were making a smoothie.

Pour the mixture into a bowl and stir in the chia seeds. Cover and refrigerate for 30 minutes. Give the mixture a good stir so the seeds don't stick together. Refrigerate for another 30 minutes, or for up to 1 day.

Scoop into small bowls and serve.

vanilla bean and banana affogato

MAKES ABOUT THREE CUPS [720 G]

This is a great story of "sweet meets coffee"—the perfect blend for an afternoon pick-me-up or an after-dinner treat. I have an espresso maker, but you could also make espresso at home with instant espresso and hot water. Just follow the package directions.

3 or 4 ripe bananas, sliced

1 vanilla bean, split

1 to 2 Tbsp unsweetened almond or cashew milk, if needed

Fresh hot espresso for serving

Arrange the banana slices on a baking sheet and freeze until firm, 30 to 45 minutes. Transfer the slices to a large zippered plastic bag and freeze overnight. (Freezing them helps the slices not to all freeze in one large lump, which will help with blending later.)

Scrape the vanilla seeds from the pod using the tip of a small sharp knife. In a food processor or blender, combine the frozen banana slices and vanilla seeds. Blend to a soft-serve consistency. If the mixture won't get smooth, add a Tbsp of almond or cashew milk to thin it.

Freeze in an airtight container. The mixture will go from soft-serve to frozen ice cream consistency, so allow it to thaw for a few minutes before you're ready to scoop.

To make an affogato, simply put a big scoop of the banana ice cream in a glass or coffee cup (glass looks pretty, though) and pour a hot shot of espresso over the top. Serve immediately, as the ice cream will begin to melt right away— which is a good thing!

mango-coconut ice cream

MAKES ONE QUART [1 L]

This ice cream can be made with any number of different fruits. I make it most often with mango, but peaches or strawberries are terrific, too. If possible, choose a fruit that is in season or was at the time it was frozen, as it will have a better overall flavor. Whatever you end up using, you'll be glad to have a small container of Weekday ice cream in your freezer to get you through those moments when you want to reach for something sweet, but don't want to wreck your eating plan.

If your can of coconut milk is cold when you begin making this ice cream (sometimes I store mine in the refrigerator to make coconut whipped cream, see page 39), then you may want to heat this on the stove so it's very smooth and no bits of coconut fat are left floating in the liquid. You want the ice cream base to blend into complete smoothness.

1 vanilla bean, split
1 can [13½ oz/385 g] full-fat coconut milk (see recipe introduction)
3 cups [420 g] frozen cubed mango
1 Tbsp raw honey or pure maple syrup
1 to 2 Tbsp unsweetened almond milk or water, if needed
Chopped nuts for serving (optional)

Scrape the vanilla seeds from the pod using the tip of a small, sharp knife. In a blender or food processor, combine the coconut milk (cream and liquid) and vanilla seeds and blend until very smooth.

Add the frozen mango and honey. Pulse until you have a soft-serve consistency. If the mixture is too thick to blend well, add a Tbsp of almond milk or water. You can enjoy some of this right then, if you like. What you don't consume, freeze in a small airtight container.

When ready to serve, let the ice cream stand at room temperature for a minute. Scoop into small bowls and serve, topped with chopped nuts or fresh fruit, if you like.

za'atar nuts

MAKES TWO CUPS [280 G]

Baked nuts are one of life's perfect snacks, because they are filling, savory, and deliver a protein boost. These are made super delicious by lightly roasting and coating in za'atar. Even if this spice blend is new to you, don't be afraid to buy a small jar, because you will likely want to make these nuts again. Za'atar is also delicious sprinkled over all sorts of things like hummus or Baked Falafel (page 85). This is a great snack for those midafternoon hunger moments, or to have on hand for you or your significant other to snack on while dinner is being made. You can easily double this recipe for a good supply; just be sure to have a large enough pan so the nuts can be spread in one layer as they bake.

2 cups [about 280 g] raw nuts such as almonds, cashews, walnuts, and pecans, in any combination

1 Tbsp olive oil or melted coconut oil

½ tsp salt

2 Tbsp za'atar

Preheat the oven to 400°F [200°C].

In a bowl, toss the nuts with the olive oil and salt.

Put the nuts on a baking sheet lined with parchment paper and spread in a single layer. Bake for 4 minutes.

Remove from the oven, pour back into the same bowl (be careful—they will be hot), and toss in the za'atar. Then return the spiced nuts to the baking sheet, spread out again, and continue to bake until lightly browned and extremely fragrant, 4 to 5 minutes longer.

Let cool completely. Store in a zippered plastic bag or an airtight container at room temperature for up to 5 days.

easy cheesy popcorn

SERVES TWO

To say my husband and I are movie lovers is an understatement. We probably see a movie at one of the theaters in town at least twice a month on average. And we watch movies even more at home but I won't say how much because, well, this could get embarrassing. Of course one of the fun things about going to the theater is movie-theater popcorn! It's a fun treat although, admittedly, not a healthy snack in the least. At home we make popcorn often, and it's great to have a healthy alternative that is still packed with flavor. This recipe is extra fun because it involves turmeric. The color is vibrant (and makes this recipe look even more like buttery movie-theater popcorn), the flavor is interesting, and turmeric has an impressive array of health benefits, as well, including anti-inflammatory superpowers. If it's a spice you don't use often, I highly recommend it for this recipe, and then you should go Google some other turmeric recipes to try.

We make popcorn often, so we own an air popper that makes this a breeze. But feel free to use other methods to pop your popcorn if you don't own an air popper.

3 tsp sesame oil

2 tsp olive oil

¾ tsp ground turmeric

⅓ cup [65 g] popcorn, popped by any means you prefer

2 Tbsp nutritional yeast (see Note, page 127)

Salt and freshly ground pepper

In a small bowl, stir together the oils and turmeric. As soon as the popcorn is popped (and still hot), drizzle this over all the popcorn and stir or toss to try and coat as many pieces as you can. Immediately sprinkle in the nutritional yeast and toss to coat as well. The goal is to try and get some oil mixture and nutritional yeast onto every piece. Sprinkle on a little salt and black pepper as well.

If for some reason you don't eat all this popcorn in one sitting, you can store in a zippered plastic bag and enjoy within the next day or two.

WEEKEND

YESSSSSSS!!!!! It's the weekend, so it's time for a much-deserved treat after a whole week of eating well! Sometimes I crave a classic treat, the kind of thing my mom would bake when I was growing up. But I also love to try new things so many of the treats I'll share with you here are just a little different, but still totally treat-worthy. Whatever you make, take your time to enjoy it! Seriously, you deserve something sweet after all the label reading that we had to do together during the week. It's time for chocolate, butter, and sugar. Let's do this.

golden crème brûlée

SERVES SIX

J'adore crème brûlée, so I always knew that I had to share a favorite version with you. It's such an amazing dessert—and it's incredibly easy to make. I especially love making these the day before, so I can pull them out and brûlée to totally impress dinner guests, or just for a special treat. This dish feels appropriate in just about any season (I suspect because it has both cold and warm elements to it). You can dress it up with fresh fruit or whipped cream. And I am such a sucker for any custard- or pudding-textured dish— it just feels so decadent to me. This version features spicy turmeric and ginger flavors that contrast with the creaminess of this dessert. I truly think a small kitchen torch works best to brûlée these, but if you don't want to buy one, I get it. An oven broiler will also work, although may not cook as evenly as a torch, but it will certainly get the job done. If you don't have a kitchen torch or an oven, well, you're out of luck on this one.

As I said above, this is a great make-ahead dessert. You can make the custards days in advance and simply store, covered, in the refrigerator. The turmeric and ginger flavors will deepen over time. I once served these 3 days after I had made the custards—I know, I was pushing it—and they were still very delicious, as the flavors were even more pronounced than when served the day after the custards are made.

⅔ cup [130 g] granulated sugar

¾ tsp ground turmeric

¾ tsp ground ginger

6 large egg yolks
 (see Note, page 167)

3½ cups [840 ml] heavy cream

Freshly ground pepper

3 tsp superfine sugar or
 granulated sugar

Preheat the oven to 325°F [165°C]. Place six 6-oz [175-ml] ramekins in a large baking dish or casserole.

In a large bowl, preferably with a pouring spout, whisk together the ⅔ cup [130 g] granulated sugar, the turmeric, and the ginger. Whisk in the egg yolks. Don't overmix, but do feel free to whisk so that everything is well blended.

continued . . .

Slowly pour in the cream, whisking to incorporate it. Pour the very wet mixture into the ramekins, dividing it evenly. Carefully fill the baking dish with enough water to come up the sides of the ramekins by 1 in [2.5 cm]. The water bath regulates the temperature so the eggs cook slowly and evenly.

Carefully transfer to the oven and bake for 45 to 50 minutes. The custards should still have quite a bit of jiggle to them, but they should be beginning to set along the edges. Remove from the oven and let cool. Cover and refrigerate for at least 3 hours, but for best results I like to refrigerate overnight, or for up to 2 days. If you don't let the custards completely cool, the centers may still be runny when you serve, so it's important to be very patient.

To brûlée with a kitchen torch, top each custard with a sprinkle of pepper and ½ tsp of the superfine sugar. Pass the torch slowly in small, circular motions across the surface of the custard about 3 in [7½ cm] above it, until the top begins to brown and starts to bubble. You're aiming to caramelize the sugar but you don't want to hold the torch so closely that it warms the custard underneath too much.

To brûlée under the broiler, preheat the broiler. Top each custard with a sprinkle of pepper and ½ tsp of the superfine sugar. Place on a baking sheet. Place under the broiler on high. After 30 seconds, check to see how they are doing. It may take 1 to 1½ minutes to broil each top until brown and bubbly looking. It's best to hover and check often to make sure you don't burn the brûlée; also, many ovens have hotter spots then others, so you may want to (carefully, wearing oven mitts!) rotate your pan partway through to get everything as evenly caramelized as possible.

Let cool for about 1 minute, then serve. My favorite part of crème brulee is cracking the sugar top just before eating. It's fun and results in such a weird blend of textures: a crunchy caramelized top with a creamy, smooth custard.

Note: Separate the egg yolks from the whites in two separate bowls, just in case you have any shell pieces you need to pluck out. Save your egg whites and make an egg white omelet or meringue later. It's just too sad to throw them all out, isn't it? You can cover and save them in the refrigerator for a few days.

167

A Beautiful Mess

sesame, sea salt, and dark chocolate cookies

MAKES TWO DOZEN COOKIES

You'll note that I use some whole-wheat flour in this recipe even though it's the weekend. The madness! No, actually you really won't be able to detect the difference much at all so why not add a touch of nutrition. Plus we already have whole-wheat flour in our pantries from the weekdays so why not use it? We're still getting plenty of butter and sugar so no need to even notice that little bit of whole-wheat flour. Please note, this make 2 dozen small cookies, so have a plan to share, or bake at your own risk.

Enjoy these warm, with a tall glass of milk. It could even be whole milk, if you dare. It's the weekend, baby!

1 cup [140 g] all-purpose flour

½ cup [70 g] white whole-wheat flour

1 tsp salt

¾ tsp aluminum-free baking powder

½ cup [110 g] unsalted butter, softened

½ cup [90 g] packed brown sugar

¼ cup [50 g] granulated sugar

1 tsp pure vanilla extract

1 large egg

1 cup [180 g] dark chocolate chips

2 to 3 Tbsp sesame seeds

2 to 3 tsp coarse sea salt (optional; my favorite for these cookies is Maldon)

Preheat the oven to 350°F [180°C]. Line a baking sheet with parchment paper or a silicone baking mat.

In a medium bowl, whisk together the flours, salt, and baking powder.

In a large bowl, cream together the butter and sugars until well combined. Stir in the vanilla and egg. Add the flour mixture and stir until a dough ball forms. Fold in the chocolate chips. Refrigerate the dough for at least 30 minutes, or for up to 2 days.

Divide the dough into 24 small balls, each about 2 Tbsp. Pour the sesame seeds onto a plate. Roll each dough ball in the seeds and place on the prepared baking sheet. Sprinkle each cookie with the coarse salt, if using.

Bake for 12 minutes, or until the edges begin to brown. Transfer the sheet to a wire cooling rack and let cool on the sheet for 5 minutes, then transfer the cookies to the rack. Serve warm.

peanut butter and plantain cookies

MAKES EIGHTEEN COOKIES

Plantains aren't an item that ends up in my grocery bags often. We consume a lot more bananas at our house than we do plantains. Probably the dark, blackened skins of plantains kept me away for so long, but I finally started exploring them, and found the main difference between the two is that plantains are less sweet and starchier than bananas, which lends them versatility for both sweet and savory dishes. In this recipe, they add a subtle flavor and help keep the center of the cookies soft and chewy, even well after they've been baked. You can leave these plantain cookies mainly plain, or add some chopped nuts or semisweet chocolate chips to the batter. They are delicious any way—but I usually add a little chocolate!

1 ripe plantain (see Note, page 172)

½ cup [110 g] unsalted butter, softened

½ cup [100 g] granulated sugar

¼ cup [45 g] packed brown sugar

⅓ cup [85 g] peanut butter

1 large egg

1 tsp pure vanilla extract

1 cup [140 g] all-purpose flour

½ tsp aluminum-free baking powder

¼ tsp salt

½ cup chocolate chips [90 g] or chopped nuts [70 g] (optional)

Preheat the oven to 350°F [180°C]. Line baking sheet with parchment paper or a silicone baking mat.

Peel the plantain and mash in a small bowl.

In a large bowl or stand mixer, beat together the butter and sugars until well blended. Add the peanut butter, mashed plantain, egg, and vanilla and stir until well combined.

In a separate bowl, whisk together the flour, baking powder, and salt. Add the dry ingredients to the wet ingredients and stir until a dough ball begins to form. Stir in the chocolate or nuts, if using, then cover with plastic wrap and refrigerate for at least an hour or for up to 2 days.

continued . . .

Scoop 2-Tbsp portions of dough onto the prepared sheet. Use a fork to gently press the dough down, so the cookie dough is flattened slightly and won't cook into a high dome.

Bake for 12 to 13 minutes. The edges and bottoms of the cookies should be beginning to brown, but the centers will still be quite soft. Transfer the sheet to a wire cooling rack and let cool on the sheet for 5 minutes, then transfer the cookies to the rack and let cool completely.

Store in an airtight container for up to 3 days.

Note: Plantains are edible at various stages in their ripening. In the tart, acidic, very firm green stage, they are used for chips in Latin cuisine; yellow plantains are still firm and starchy and are often diced for soups and stews, like a potato. When the skin is mostly black but with spots of yellow and the flesh yields to light pressure like a ripe peach, the plantain is fully ripe—perfect for baked goods like this recipe. You are more likely to find plantains in the green or yellow state at the market, so place them in a paper bag until they're where you want them. Even a totally black and mushy plantain is delicious in cooking and baking, without the excessive sweetness of an overripe banana.

If your plantain isn't super ripe—that is, still showing a lot of yellow and not easily mashed with a fork—preheat the oven to 400°F [200°C]. Place the plantain on a baking sheet and roast for 20 minutes. This will bring out more flavor and caramelize the sugars a bit. If you have one that is very ripe and ready to mash, skip this step.

double-chocolate surprise brownies

MAKES NINE LARGE OR TWELVE SMALL BROWNIES

This is the kind of dessert I will fantasize about all week and that's because—chocolate! And this recipe does not disappoint. These brownies have a dense, cakelike crumb that is moist but not gooey. It's also very chocolaty but not overly sweet, making these perfect for topping with a scoop of vanilla ice cream or dusting with a little powdered sugar. Or just pour yourself a tall glass of milk.

So, what's the surprise? These also have a whole zucchini baked into them, which adds moisture more than flavor, in my opinion. Give them a try—I think you'll also be surprised by how much you love them!

1 large zucchini, about 6 oz [170 g], peeled and chopped

⅓ cup [85 g] unsalted butter, melted and cooled

2 large eggs

1½ tsp pure vanilla extract

¼ cup [50 g] sugar

¼ cup [45 g] brown sugar

⅔ cup [50 g] Dutch-processed cocoa

½ tsp aluminum-free baking powder

¼ tsp salt

¾ cup [105 g] all-purpose flour

½ cup [90 g] dark or semi-sweet chocolate chips

Candied fruits and nuts (optional)

Preheat the oven to 350°F [180°C].

Put the zucchini in a food processor until well blended. The zucchini should be almost a very thick juice at this point. You don't want any large pieces, as these will be perceptible in your brownie batter and ruin the surprise.

In a large bowl, stir together the zucchini, butter, eggs, vanilla, and sugars until just blended.

In a medium bowl, whisk together the cocoa, baking powder, salt, and flour. Add the dry ingredients to the wet ingredients in two batches, stirring after each addition until nearly no lumps remain. Fold in the chocolate chips.

continued . . .

Pour the batter into an 8-in [20-cm] square baking pan lined with parchment paper. Top with candied fruit, if desired. Bake until a toothpick inserted into the center comes out clean, 20 to 25 minutes. The brownies will continue to bake a little after you pull them out, so don't be afraid if a few crumbs are clinging to the toothpick, or the center still seems soft; you just don't want any raw batter left.

Let cool for a few minutes in the pan, then carefully lift from the pan and move to a cutting board. Slice into small squares and enjoy while they are still warm.

To store any leftovers (as if!), wrap individually in plastic wrap and pack in an airtight container. I like to briefly rewarm next-day brownies in the microwave for a couple seconds.

best berry cobbler

SERVES FOUR

This tastes exactly like summer to me. We've been going berry picking with our mom since we were little girls. And everyone knows that the real reward of berry picking is cobbler—sweet, sticky cobbler served with a big scoop of vanilla ice cream, preferably eaten outdoors while the sun is starting to set and fireflies are just starting to come out. I love summer, and I love this cobbler. It's just too easy to make and so delicious. And as one recipe tester told me, if you have leftovers it makes a great weekend breakfast topped with Greek yogurt, too.

¼ cup [55 g] unsalted butter, softened, plus more for greasing

½ cup [100 g] sugar

½ tsp pure vanilla extract

½ cup [70 g] all-purpose flour (it will still be delicious if you want to use white whole-wheat flour here instead)

½ tsp aluminum-free baking powder

¼ tsp salt

1⅓ cups [185 g] blueberries

1⅓ cups [160 g] blackberries

Zest of 1 lemon

Vanilla ice cream for serving

Preheat the oven to 375°F [190°C].

In a bowl, combine the butter, sugar, and vanilla and beat until well combined. Add the flour, baking powder, and salt and stir until a crumbly dough forms.

Lightly butter a pie pan and fill with the berries. Scatter the lemon zest on top. Sprinkle the crumble top all over the berries.

Bake until the berries begin to bubble and the crumble top begins to brown, 30 to 35 minutes. Serve warm with a scoop of ice cream on top.

dri

from the nutritionists

Most people do not consume enough water. On average, a grown person requires at least 64 ounces (or 8 cups) of water each day. This will vary based on activity level and body size. For every cup or glass (one cup = 8 oz) of caffeinated beverage consumed, drinking one glass of water or non-caffeinated beverage is recommended to replace fluids. Fruit-infused waters or decaffeinated teas are great for increasing fluid intake while not filling up on excessive sugars or caffeine.

Diet Soda

If you are reading a cookbook and therefore interested in good food, we assume you already know that sweet drinks such as Kool-Aid, sodas, and energy drinks are sources of empty calories and to be avoided in your weekday diet. As dietitians we discourage the consumption of artificial sweeteners, which are a main ingredient in diet drinks. Not only are they unnatural, but the fact is we really don't know the long-term effects these ingredients can have on our bodies. Just because something says zero calories does not make it "good for you." Plus, your brain still gets the message you are consuming sweets, so you will crave more. Are we really fixing anything or just putting a Band-Aid on an underlying sweet addiction? We emphasize increasing the good: waters, herbal blends, unsweetened teas. Drink these and be merry while avoiding the diet drinks if you can.

Coffee and Tea

In recent years, studies have continued to find many positive health benefits of coffees, teas, and herbal blends. When consumed in moderation, coffee may protect against many chronic diseases and promote heart health. Tea helps to protect bones and boost the immune system, all while providing antioxidant benefits.

Cocktails and Spirits

When the weekend rolls around, put your feet up and celebrate a week of successful eating with a cocktail if that's your thing. These recipes include delicious and healthy herbs and antioxidant-rich fruits to balance the booze.

easy, homemade sun tea

Sun tea is a summer tradition in my family. Each time I make it, I am transported back to my childhood in southern Missouri, with my mom in bare feet on the front porch. My favorite: unsweetened peach tea with lemon slices and a few fresh mint leaves.

To make sun tea, fill a 32-oz [960-ml] glass pitcher or oversized jar with water. Add 3 tea bags and a handful of fruit or herbs to the water. Cover the top with a clean kitchen towel (or anything to keep bugs out) and let it sit in the sunshine on your porch for a couple of hours. It's that simple!

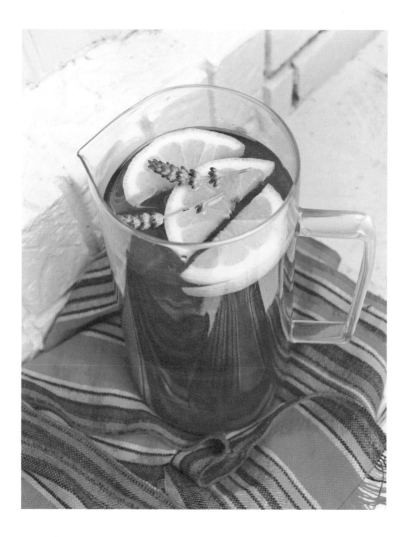

A Beautiful Mess

twelve ideas for infused waters

Infused waters (or "spa waters" as I like to call them) are a great way to motivate yourself to drink more water throughout the day. Let's just be honest: water is boring. But spa water? Well, that's another story!

Elevate your daily H_2O with herbs and fruit. Prepare yourself a giant pitcher in the morning and you'll be amazed how easy it is to drink a lot of water throughout the day. Just add 1 to 2 handfuls to a 32-oz [960-ml] pitcher and allow to infuse for at least 30 minutes; the longer you allow the mixture to infuse the stronger the flavor. If you prefer chilled water add ice or let infuse in the refrigerator before enjoying.

These are a few of my favorite combinations!

- Orange and Star Anise
- Watermelon, Fresh Mint, and Fresh Basil
- Cucumber, Fresh Mint, and Lemon
- Pineapple and Orange
- Lemon, Blueberries, Blackberries, and Raspberries
- Cucumber and Strawberries
- Lime and Blueberries
- Apple and Cinnamon Sticks
- Blackberries and Fresh Mint
- Grapefruit and Fresh Rosemary
- Orange and Turmeric
- Pineapple and Ginger

fresh mint
hot chocolate

SERVES ONE

This minty hot chocolate recipe is smooth and indulgent—like sipping melted chocolate, but you can definitely taste the mint. Try it alongside a sliced orange for another fun twist!

1 cup [240 ml] whole milk

2½ oz [70 g] dark chocolate, chopped

12 fresh mint leaves, torn into
   small pieces

Combine the milk, chocolate, and mint in a saucepan over medium heat and cook, stirring until the chocolate is completely dissolved. The mint flavor will infuse as the chocolate melts. Strain into a mug and serve.

fresh apple and ginger cocktail

SERVES ONE

This apple juice-based cocktail quickly shot up to the top of my brunch cocktail list—it's even better than a mimosa! Try it for something different and unexpected next time you host a brunch party. The tart and sweet combination is one of my absolute favorites. If you find this is too tart to your liking you can simply try using different apples. Granny Smith apples have a sour-tart flavor that balances perfectly with the sweet and spicy liqueur, but there are many different apple varieties that could work well here. Gala apples or Honey Crisp are great options to try.

Ice
1 cup [240 ml] fresh Granny Smith
   apple juice (if you're juicing
   your own at home, you'll need
   about 3 apples)
2 oz [60 ml] ginger liqueur
   (I love Domaine De Canton)

Fill a tall glass with ice. Add the juice and liqueur and stir. Serve immediately.

hibiscus-margarita
snow cones

SERVES TWO

In need of a wow-factor cocktail? This boozy margarita is delicious, special,
and so much fun to make. Add a striped straw for a final festive flourish,
if you like.

1½ oz [45 ml] Hibiscus Tequila
  (recipe follows)
1 oz [30 ml] triple sec
4 oz [120 ml] Margarita Mix
  (recipe follows)
Chipped ice or shaved ice
Key lime slices, fresh mint leaves,
  or berries for garnish

In a cocktail shaker filled with ice combine the tequila, triple sec, and margarita mix. Shake until you feel the shaker become very cold in your hands. Fill a small glass with chipped ice, creating a dome over the top. Pour the cocktail over the ice and garnish.

hibiscus tequila

6 oz [135 ml] tequila
1 hibiscus tea bag

Pour the tequila into a glass measuring cup, add the tea bag, and let steep for 1 hour.

margarita mix

1 cup [240 ml] fresh lime juice
  (from about 10 limes)
1 cup [240 ml] water
½ cup [100 g] sugar

Squeeze the lime juice into a bowl or measuring cup. Heat the water and sugar in a saucepan over medium heat until the sugar has dissolved. Let the mixture cool a bit before adding in the lime juice, mix together, and pour into a bottle. Refrigerate the mix for up to 2 weeks.

A Beautiful Mess

blended watermelon mojitos

SERVES TWO

The mojito holds a special place in my heart, because it was my first go-to cocktail. This version infuses fresh summer flavors for something truly refreshing. The perfect cocktail for those long summer nights.

2 cups [280 g] cubed
   seedless watermelon
4 oz [120 ml] light rum
¼ cup [60 ml] simple syrup
   (recipe follows)
Juice and zest of 1 lime,
   plus 2 twists for garnish
12 fresh mint leaves,
   plus more for garnish
2 cups [280 g] ice cubes

Combine all of the ingredients in a blender and process on high until blended and smooth. Divide between 2 tall glasses or fill the inside of half a small watermelon. Garnish each with a mint leaf or two and a lime twist and serve immediately.

simple syrup

Making simple syrup is as easy as boiling water. Fantastically handy for stirring into cold mixes, this liquid sweetener is great for iced coffee and teas and summer citrus ades as well as cocktails. Just a drop will often do!

1 cup [200 g] sugar
1 cup [240 ml] water

Combine the sugar and water in a small saucepan. Place over medium heat and cook, stirring to help dissolve the sugar, just until the sugar is melted and the syrup is clear, about 5 minutes. Do not let boil. Let cool, then store in a tightly covered bottle in the fridge for up to 2 weeks.

peach whiskey smash

SERVES ONE

I love any cocktail where I get to muddle fresh ingredients! This cocktail is a sweet and strong concoction with fruity flavors. This drink is for whiskey lovers only, as the flavor is very prominent.

½ ripe peach, peeled, pitted, and diced

2 Tbsp simple syrup (page 191)

4 fresh mint leaves, torn into small pieces, plus a few small leaves for serving

2 oz [60 ml] whiskey

Ice cubes

A giant ice cube, fresh mint leaves, and thin peach slices for serving

In a cocktail shaker, combine the diced peach, simple syrup, and mint leaves. Muddle together until soft and juicy. Add the whiskey and fill with ice cubes. Shake.

To serve, place a giant ice cube in a small highball glass. Strain the mixture into the glass, garnish with a few mint leaves and a peach slice or two, and serve immediately.

A Beautiful Mess

mint julep lemonade

SERVES ONE

This is a fun play on the classic mint julep.
The lemonade lightens it up and adds a twist.

2 large fresh mint leaves,
  plus a small sprig for garnish
1 oz [30 ml] mint-infused simple
  syrup (see Note)
2 oz [60 ml] bourbon, such as
  Buffalo Trace
2 oz [60 ml] fresh lemon juice
1 dash mint bitters (optional)
Ice cubes

Muddle or smash the mint leaves in the bottom of a traditional mint julep cup, highball, or any small cocktail glass; this allows them to release some oil (read: more flavor). Combine the mint simple syrup, bourbon, lemon juice, and bitters, if using, in a cocktail shaker and fill the shaker with ice. Shake vigorously until the shaker becomes very cold in your hands. Add ice to the cocktail glass (leaving the muddled leaves at the bottom) and strain the drink into the glass over the ice. Garnish with the sprig of mint and serve immediately.

Note: To make mint-infused simple syrup, make the simple syrup as instructed on page 191, adding 2 Tbsp finely chopped fresh mint to the mix before heating. After the sugar has dissolved completely, remove from the heat and let cool completely in the pan. Strain the syrup through a fine-mesh strainer into a bottle, cover tightly, and refrigerate for up to 2 weeks.

rose and tonic

SERVES ONE

Floral flavors in drinks (as with food) are tricky. When done right, they add intrigue; when done wrong, your drink tastes like perfume. This unusual and delicious recipe uses a clever technique to practice your floral-flavoring skills. Remember that a little goes a long way!

2 oz [60 ml] gin
⅔ cup [155 ml] tonic water
1 Tbsp fresh lime juice
Ice cubes
Rosewater
Lime wedge for serving

In a Collins glass, combine the gin, tonic water, and lime juice. Fill the glass with ice cubes. Using a paper straw, dip the tip of the straw into the bottle of rosewater, then use the straw to stir the drink. This tiny bit of rosewater will flavor your drink mildly, without tasting like perfume. Garnish with the lime wedge and serve immediately.

A Beautiful Mess

lavender collins

SERVES ONE

A classic Tom Collins is also one of the most classically refreshing three-ingredient cocktails: gin, lemon, and a little sugar, plus a float of sparkling water. Infuse it with lavender and it becomes a bubbly spiked lavender lemonade.

Ice cubes

2 oz [60 ml] gin

2 Tbsp lavender simple syrup (see Note)

1½ Tbsp fresh lemon juice

2 oz [60 ml] club soda

Lemon wedge for garnish

Fill a Collins glass with ice. Add the gin, simple syrup, lemon juice, and club soda and stir. Garnish with the lemon wedge and serve immediately.

Note: To make lavender simple syrup, make the simple syrup as instructed on page 191, adding 1 tsp dried lavender buds to the mix before heating. After the sugar has dissolved completely, remove from the heat and let cool completely in the pan. Strain the syrup through a fine-mesh strainer into a bottle, cover tightly, and refrigerate for up to 2 weeks.

grapefruit and elderflower cocktail

SERVES ONE

This drink packs a punch. It is flavorful, sweet, and tart. Luxardo cherries can be a little tricky to find and are more expensive than maraschino cherries, but they're worth it. Once you taste them, I promise you'll be hooked. You can add one or two and a drizzle of the juice they're packed in to club soda or seltzer for a light and delicious mocktail. Use as an ice cream topping, or just eat straight from the jar.

Ice cubes

2 oz [60 ml] fresh grapefruit juice, strained

2 oz [60 ml] St-Germain Elderflower Liqueur

1 Tbsp Luxardo cherry syrup

2 Luxardo cherries

Grapefruit wedge for garnish (optional)

Fill a cocktail shaker with ice. Pour in the grapefruit juice, St-Germain, and cherry syrup. Shake vigorously until the shaker feels very cold in your hands. Strain into a martini glass or coupe, drop in the cherries, and garnish with a grapefruit wedge, if you like. Serve immediately.

resources

There are SO many great resources to pull from if you are looking to make delicious food that can work along with the Weekday Weekend eating challenge. The majority of the folks we are listing here have written books, articles, blog posts, and even long Instagram posts that can provide more inspiration for healthy options during the week. But we've also included some folks who just make amazing food that would need to fall under weekend treats more often than not. They are all worth checking out, if you haven't already:

- Adriana Adarme
- Tracy Benjamin
- Mark Bittman
- Sophie Bourdon
- Kim Boyce
- Sarah Britton
- Jeni Britton Bauer
- Andrea Duclos
- David and Stephen Flynn
- Sara and Will Forte
- Donna Hay
- McKel Hill
- David Lebovitz
- Angela Liddon
- Tara O'Brady
- Jamie Oliver
- Lindsay Ostrom
- Deb Perelman
- Dana Shultz
- Heidi Swanson
- Julia Turshen
- Joy Wilson

What about some shopping resources?

Schoolhouseelectric.com has an incredible selection of really nice serving pieces.

CB2.com is amazing for cute dishes and glasses and adorable prices.

Leifshop.com is a great resource for trendy, curated tabletop items.

Shop.OhHappyDay.com is our favorite one-stop for party items.

Turkish-T by Sue Joyce for luxurious table linens, many of which are pictured throughout this book (in case you're curious).

Askinosie Chocolate makes amazing chocolate (for your weekends) and they do right by their farmers as well.

Themasonbarcompany.com sells great containers for making infused waters.

A Beautiful Mess

thank you

Thank you to our husbands, Jeremy and Trey, for putting up with all our very first test recipes and all the dirty dishes this book created along the way. Your love, support, and honest interest in our work always inspires us to keep going, even when we feel like we don't know what we're doing.

Thank you, Mom and Dad, for all the love, encouragement, and homemade meals that we received growing up. You both inspire us to keep creating and to enjoy the good things in life with joy and passion.

Thank you, Laura Gummerman, for your continued assistance, honest feedback, and occasional grocery store runs. When we think about how we are able to accomplish big projects like this you are one of the very first people that comes to mind. You are the real secret weapon.

Thank you, Lindsay Edgecombe, for being our agent and the voice of reason during phone meetings. You've stood by us for all three books we've put together, and your guidance has made each one better.

Thank you, Sarah Billingsley, our kind and honest editor, Carrie Bradley Neves, as well as the whole team at Chronicle Books. Thank you for believing in this book and for helping us to bring it to life. We are so, so glad you gave us a chance to write a cookbook!

Thank you, Sarah O'Callaghan and Lindsey Kelsay, for agreeing to consult and help shape this book from a nutritionist's point of view. The information and advice you provided helped us on our own healthy eating journey, and we know it is sure to help many readers as well.

Thank you to everyone who willingly recipe tested for us: Holly, Mara, Morgan, Laura, Mallory, Rachel, Katie, Jen, Sarah, Jacki, Michelle, and Janae. And also thank you to all the significant others, roommates, children (including our niece, Penelope), and coworkers who, although you didn't volunteer to recipe test, our testers (or we) inflicted the task on you anyway. All of the feedback you gave helped make the recipes in this book that much better!

And the last two groups we'd like to thank are made up mostly of people we've never met in real life. First, thank you to all the *A Beautiful Mess* blog readers. Your interest and continued support over the years has inspired us greatly, and still does! You push us to create our very best work and for that, we thank you from the bottom of our hearts. And we also have to thank all our fellow food bloggers, cookbook authors, foodies, chefs, and food photographers whom we admire, and who inspire us. Many of you are listed under the resources in this book because you are just that: an incredible resource. We cannot believe we have the great privilege of getting to create work alongside you guys—the thought humbles us. You all are truly amazing, and our hats are off to you.

A Beautiful Mess

about the authors

Emma Chapman and **Elsie Larson** are the entrepreneurial sister team behind the lifestyle blog *A Beautiful Mess*. Their previous books include *A Beautiful Mess Photo Idea Book* and *Happy Handmade Home*. Their work has appeared in *Domino*, *Real Simple*, and *Southern Living*, among other publications. Elsie lives in Nashville, Tennessee. Emma lives in Springfield, Missouri, where she is also a co-owner of The Golden Girl Rum Club. Visit abeautifulmess.com.

index

A Beautiful Mess

A Beautiful Mess

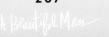

A Beautiful Mess